Just for the Middle Level

- **Test Prep Works materials are developed for a specific test and level, making it easier for students to focus on relevant content**

- **The Middle Level SSAT is for students applying for admission to grades 6-8 – see table at the end of this book for materials for other grades**

- **Two books are available from Test Prep Works to help students prepare for the Middle Level SSAT**

Success on the Middle Level SSAT: A Complete Course

- Strategies for each section of the test

- Reading and vocabulary drills

- In-depth math content instruction with practice sets

The Best Unofficial Practice Tests for the Middle Level SSAT

- 2 full-length practice tests

TEST PREP WORKS, LLC.

THE BEST *Unofficial*
PRACTICE TESTS
FOR THE Middle Level SSAT

Two full-length practice tests developed specifically for the Middle Level SSAT

Christa Abbott, M.Ed.

Published by:
Test Prep Works, LLC
PO Box 100572
Arlington, VA 22210
www.TestPrepWorks.com

For information about buying this title in bulk, or for editions with customized covers or content, please contact the publisher at sales@testprepworks.com or (703) 944-6727.

The SSAT is a registered trademark of The Enrollment Management Association, which has neither endorsed nor associated itself in any way with this book.

Neither the author nor the publisher of this book claims responsibility for the accuracy of this book or the outcome of students who use these materials.

ISBN: 978-1-939090-96-6

Contents

How To Use This Book

The tests in this book will give you an idea of the types of questions you will see, the concepts likely to be tested, and the format and timing of the test. You will also get a sense of how the scoring works – one point is given for each correct answer and a quarter point is subtracted for each incorrect answer.

Try to work through the test in "real conditions" to get a sense of what it feels like to take a test of this length, which may be longer than what you are used to. Be sure to time yourself on each section and stop when the time is up, just like you will have to on test day.

The following chart lays out the general timing of the test:

Section	Time
Writing Sample – choose 1 prompt	25 minutes
*** 5 minute break ***	
1st Quantitative Section – 25 questions	30 minutes
Reading Section – 40 questions	40 minutes
*** 5 minute break ***	
Verbal Section – 60 questions	30 minutes
2nd Quantitative Section – 25 questions	30 minutes

There may also be a 15-minute experimental section at the end of the actual test. These questions will NOT contribute to your score. The test writers are simply trying out new questions for a future SSAT.

After you complete a practice test, check all of your answers. Figure out WHY you missed the questions that you answered incorrectly. Think about what you would do differently if you had to answer a similar question in the future. Then, remember what you learned when you take another practice test (if you plan to) and the SSAT itself.

About Test Prep Works

Test Prep Works, LLC, was founded in 2011 to provide effective materials for test preparation. Its founder, Christa Abbott, had struggled for years to find effective materials to use with her own students for the private school entrance exams, but came up empty-handed. The books that were available combined several different tests and levels into a single set of instructional materials. There may be similarities, but they are not the same test. Christa found this to be confusing and overwhelming for her students, especially those in elementary and middle school. That seemed completely unnecessary. Christa developed her own materials to use with students that are specific to each level of the test and are not just adapted from other books. She then founded Test Prep Works in order to make these materials available to the general public as well as other tutors. You can visit www.TestPrepWorks.com to find more information about these materials.

Answer Sheets

Practice Test 1

Section 1: Quantitative		
1 (A) (B) (C) (D) (E)	10 (A) (B) (C) (D) (E)	19 (A) (B) (C) (D) (E)
2 (A) (B) (C) (D) (E)	11 (A) (B) (C) (D) (E)	20 (A) (B) (C) (D) (E)
3 (A) (B) (C) (D) (E)	12 (A) (B) (C) (D) (E)	21 (A) (B) (C) (D) (E)
4 (A) (B) (C) (D) (E)	13 (A) (B) (C) (D) (E)	22 (A) (B) (C) (D) (E)
5 (A) (B) (C) (D) (E)	14 (A) (B) (C) (D) (E)	23 (A) (B) (C) (D) (E)
6 (A) (B) (C) (D) (E)	15 (A) (B) (C) (D) (E)	24 (A) (B) (C) (D) (E)
7 (A) (B) (C) (D) (E)	16 (A) (B) (C) (D) (E)	25 (A) (B) (C) (D) (E)
8 (A) (B) (C) (D) (E)	17 (A) (B) (C) (D) (E)	
9 (A) (B) (C) (D) (E)	18 (A) (B) (C) (D) (E)	

Section 2: Reading Comprehension		
1 (A) (B) (C) (D) (E)	15 (A) (B) (C) (D) (E)	29 (A) (B) (C) (D) (E)
2 (A) (B) (C) (D) (E)	16 (A) (B) (C) (D) (E)	30 (A) (B) (C) (D) (E)
3 (A) (B) (C) (D) (E)	17 (A) (B) (C) (D) (E)	31 (A) (B) (C) (D) (E)
4 (A) (B) (C) (D) (E)	18 (A) (B) (C) (D) (E)	32 (A) (B) (C) (D) (E)
5 (A) (B) (C) (D) (E)	19 (A) (B) (C) (D) (F)	33 (A) (B) (C) (D) (E)
6 (A) (B) (C) (D) (E)	20 (A) (B) (C) (D) (E)	34 (A) (B) (C) (D) (E)
7 (A) (B) (C) (D) (E)	21 (A) (B) (C) (D) (E)	35 (A) (B) (C) (D) (E)
8 (A) (B) (C) (D) (E)	22 (A) (B) (C) (D) (E)	36 (A) (B) (C) (D) (E)
9 (A) (B) (C) (D) (E)	23 (A) (B) (C) (D) (E)	37 (A) (B) (C) (D) (E)
10 (A) (B) (C) (D) (E)	24 (A) (B) (C) (D) (E)	38 (A) (B) (C) (D) (E)
11 (A) (B) (C) (D) (E)	25 (A) (B) (C) (D) (E)	39 (A) (B) (C) (D) (E)
12 (A) (B) (C) (D) (E)	26 (A) (B) (C) (D) (E)	40 (A) (B) (C) (D) (E)
13 (A) (B) (C) (D) (E)	27 (A) (B) (C) (D) (E)	
14 (A) (B) (C) (D) (E)	28 (A) (B) (C) (D) (E)	

Section 3: Verbal		
1 (A) (B) (C) (D) (E)	21 (A) (B) (C) (D) (E)	41 (A) (B) (C) (D) (E)
2 (A) (B) (C) (D) (E)	22 (A) (B) (C) (D) (E)	42 (A) (B) (C) (D) (E)
3 (A) (B) (C) (D) (E)	23 (A) (B) (C) (D) (E)	43 (A) (B) (C) (D) (E)
4 (A) (B) (C) (D) (E)	24 (A) (B) (C) (D) (E)	44 (A) (B) (C) (D) (E)
5 (A) (B) (C) (D) (E)	25 (A) (B) (C) (D) (E)	45 (A) (B) (C) (D) (E)
6 (A) (B) (C) (D) (E)	26 (A) (B) (C) (D) (E)	46 (A) (B) (C) (D) (E)
7 (A) (B) (C) (D) (E)	27 (A) (B) (C) (D) (E)	47 (A) (B) (C) (D) (E)
8 (A) (B) (C) (D) (E)	28 (A) (B) (C) (D) (E)	48 (A) (B) (C) (D) (E)
9 (A) (B) (C) (D) (E)	29 (A) (B) (C) (D) (E)	49 (A) (B) (C) (D) (E)
10 (A) (B) (C) (D) (E)	30 (A) (B) (C) (D) (E)	50 (A) (B) (C) (D) (E)
11 (A) (B) (C) (D) (E)	31 (A) (B) (C) (D) (E)	51 (A) (B) (C) (D) (E)
12 (A) (B) (C) (D) (E)	32 (A) (B) (C) (D) (E)	52 (A) (B) (C) (D) (E)
13 (A) (B) (C) (D) (E)	33 (A) (B) (C) (D) (E)	53 (A) (B) (C) (D) (E)
14 (A) (B) (C) (D) (E)	34 (A) (B) (C) (D) (E)	54 (A) (B) (C) (D) (E)
15 (A) (B) (C) (D) (E)	35 (A) (B) (C) (D) (E)	55 (A) (B) (C) (D) (E)
16 (A) (B) (C) (D) (E)	36 (A) (B) (C) (D) (E)	56 (A) (B) (C) (D) (E)
17 (A) (B) (C) (D) (E)	37 (A) (B) (C) (D) (E)	57 (A) (B) (C) (D) (E)
18 (A) (B) (C) (D) (E)	38 (A) (B) (C) (D) (E)	58 (A) (B) (C) (D) (E)
19 (A) (B) (C) (D) (E)	39 (A) (B) (C) (D) (E)	59 (A) (B) (C) (D) (E)
20 (A) (B) (C) (D) (E)	40 (A) (B) (C) (D) (E)	60 (A) (B) (C) (D) (E)

Section 4: Quantitative		
1 (A) (B) (C) (D) (E)	10 (A) (B) (C) (D) (E)	19 (A) (B) (C) (D) (E)
2 (A) (B) (C) (D) (E)	11 (A) (B) (C) (D) (E)	20 (A) (B) (C) (D) (E)
3 (A) (B) (C) (D) (E)	12 (A) (B) (C) (D) (E)	21 (A) (B) (C) (D) (E)
4 (A) (B) (C) (D) (E)	13 (A) (B) (C) (D) (E)	22 (A) (B) (C) (D) (E)
5 (A) (B) (C) (D) (E)	14 (A) (B) (C) (D) (E)	23 (A) (B) (C) (D) (E)
6 (A) (B) (C) (D) (E)	15 (A) (B) (C) (D) (E)	24 (A) (B) (C) (D) (E)
7 (A) (B) (C) (D) (E)	16 (A) (B) (C) (D) (E)	25 (A) (B) (C) (D) (E)
8 (A) (B) (C) (D) (E)	17 (A) (B) (C) (D) (E)	
9 (A) (B) (C) (D) (E)	18 (A) (B) (C) (D) (E)	

Practice Test 2

Section 1: Quantitative		
1 (A) (B) (C) (D) (E)	10 (A) (B) (C) (D) (E)	19 (A) (B) (C) (D) (E)
2 (A) (B) (C) (D) (E)	11 (A) (B) (C) (D) (E)	20 (A) (B) (C) (D) (E)
3 (A) (B) (C) (D) (E)	12 (A) (B) (C) (D) (E)	21 (A) (B) (C) (D) (E)
4 (A) (B) (C) (D) (E)	13 (A) (B) (C) (D) (E)	22 (A) (B) (C) (D) (E)
5 (A) (B) (C) (D) (E)	14 (A) (B) (C) (D) (E)	23 (A) (B) (C) (D) (E)
6 (A) (B) (C) (D) (E)	15 (A) (B) (C) (D) (E)	24 (A) (B) (C) (D) (E)
7 (A) (B) (C) (D) (E)	16 (A) (B) (C) (D) (E)	25 (A) (B) (C) (D) (E)
8 (A) (B) (C) (D) (E)	17 (A) (B) (C) (D) (E)	
9 (A) (B) (C) (D) (E)	18 (A) (B) (C) (D) (E)	

Section 2: Reading Comprehension		
1 (A) (B) (C) (D) (E)	15 (A) (B) (C) (D) (E)	29 (A) (B) (C) (D) (E)
2 (A) (B) (C) (D) (E)	16 (A) (B) (C) (D) (E)	30 (A) (B) (C) (D) (E)
3 (A) (B) (C) (D) (E)	17 (A) (B) (C) (D) (E)	31 (A) (B) (C) (D) (E)
4 (A) (B) (C) (D) (E)	18 (A) (B) (C) (D) (E)	32 (A) (B) (C) (D) (E)
5 (A) (B) (C) (D) (E)	19 (A) (B) (C) (D) (E)	33 (A) (B) (C) (D) (E)
6 (A) (B) (C) (D) (E)	20 (A) (B) (C) (D) (E)	34 (A) (B) (C) (D) (E)
7 (A) (B) (C) (D) (E)	21 (A) (B) (C) (D) (E)	35 (A) (B) (C) (D) (E)
8 (A) (B) (C) (D) (E)	22 (A) (B) (C) (D) (E)	36 (A) (B) (C) (D) (E)
9 (A) (B) (C) (D) (E)	23 (A) (B) (C) (D) (E)	37 (A) (B) (C) (D) (E)
10 (A) (B) (C) (D) (E)	24 (A) (B) (C) (D) (E)	38 (A) (B) (C) (D) (E)
11 (A) (B) (C) (D) (E)	25 (A) (B) (C) (D) (E)	39 (A) (B) (C) (D) (E)
12 (A) (B) (C) (D) (E)	26 (A) (B) (C) (D) (E)	40 (A) (B) (C) (D) (E)
13 (A) (B) (C) (D) (E)	27 (A) (B) (C) (D) (E)	
14 (A) (B) (C) (D) (E)	28 (A) (B) (C) (D) (E)	

Section 3: Verbal

1 (A) (B) (C) (D) (E)	21 (A) (B) (C) (D) (E)	41 (A) (B) (C) (D) (E)
2 (A) (B) (C) (D) (E)	22 (A) (B) (C) (D) (E)	42 (A) (B) (C) (D) (E)
3 (A) (B) (C) (D) (E)	23 (A) (B) (C) (D) (E)	43 (A) (B) (C) (D) (E)
4 (A) (B) (C) (D) (E)	24 (A) (B) (C) (D) (E)	44 (A) (B) (C) (D) (E)
5 (A) (B) (C) (D) (E)	25 (A) (B) (C) (D) (E)	45 (A) (B) (C) (D) (E)
6 (A) (B) (C) (D) (E)	26 (A) (B) (C) (D) (E)	46 (A) (B) (C) (D) (E)
7 (A) (B) (C) (D) (E)	27 (A) (B) (C) (D) (E)	47 (A) (B) (C) (D) (E)
8 (A) (B) (C) (D) (E)	28 (A) (B) (C) (D) (E)	48 (A) (B) (C) (D) (E)
9 (A) (B) (C) (D) (E)	29 (A) (B) (C) (D) (E)	49 (A) (B) (C) (D) (E)
10 (A) (B) (C) (D) (E)	30 (A) (B) (C) (D) (E)	50 (A) (B) (C) (D) (E)
11 (A) (B) (C) (D) (E)	31 (A) (B) (C) (D) (E)	51 (A) (B) (C) (D) (E)
12 (A) (B) (C) (D) (E)	32 (A) (B) (C) (D) (E)	52 (A) (B) (C) (D) (E)
13 (A) (B) (C) (D) (E)	33 (A) (B) (C) (D) (E)	53 (A) (B) (C) (D) (E)
14 (A) (B) (C) (D) (E)	34 (A) (B) (C) (D) (E)	54 (A) (B) (C) (D) (E)
15 (A) (B) (C) (D) (E)	35 (A) (B) (C) (D) (E)	55 (A) (B) (C) (D) (E)
16 (A) (B) (C) (D) (E)	36 (A) (B) (C) (D) (E)	56 (A) (B) (C) (D) (E)
17 (A) (B) (C) (D) (E)	37 (A) (B) (C) (D) (E)	57 (A) (B) (C) (D) (E)
18 (A) (B) (C) (D) (E)	38 (A) (B) (C) (D) (E)	58 (A) (B) (C) (D) (E)
19 (A) (B) (C) (D) (E)	39 (A) (B) (C) (D) (E)	59 (A) (B) (C) (D) (E)
20 (A) (B) (C) (D) (E)	40 (A) (B) (C) (D) (E)	60 (A) (B) (C) (D) (E)

Section 4: Quantitative

1 (A) (B) (C) (D) (E)	10 (A) (B) (C) (D) (E)	19 (A) (B) (C) (D) (E)
2 (A) (B) (C) (D) (E)	11 (A) (B) (C) (D) (E)	20 (A) (B) (C) (D) (E)
3 (A) (B) (C) (D) (E)	12 (A) (B) (C) (D) (E)	21 (A) (B) (C) (D) (E)
4 (A) (B) (C) (D) (E)	13 (A) (B) (C) (D) (E)	22 (A) (B) (C) (D) (E)
5 (A) (B) (C) (D) (E)	14 (A) (B) (C) (D) (E)	23 (A) (B) (C) (D) (E)
6 (A) (B) (C) (D) (E)	15 (A) (B) (C) (D) (E)	24 (A) (B) (C) (D) (E)
7 (A) (B) (C) (D) (E)	16 (A) (B) (C) (D) (E)	25 (A) (B) (C) (D) (E)
8 (A) (B) (C) (D) (E)	17 (A) (B) (C) (D) (E)	
9 (A) (B) (C) (D) (E)	18 (A) (B) (C) (D) (E)	

Practice Test 1

Writing Sample

The writing sample is a way for schools to learn a little more about you. Below are two possible writing topics. Please choose the topic that you find most interesting. Fill in the circle next to the topic you choose and then use this page and the next to write your essay.

(A)   The bright light shone in my eyes and…

(B)   I had waited for this day a long time.

Complete your writing sample on this page and the next. You have 25 minutes to complete this section.

CONTINUE TO THE NEXT PAGE

STOP

Section 1: Quantitative

25 questions
30 minutes

Directions: Each problem is followed by five answer choices. Solve each problem and then decide which answer choice is best.

---

1. Which shows 3.7847 rounded to the nearest hundredth?

    (A) 3.8
    (B) 3.78
    (C) 3.79
    (D) 3.785
    (E) 3.786

---

2. In February, Carla's Candy Shop sold y gift baskets. In March, it sold 11 more gift baskets than it had in February. In April, it sold 5 fewer gift baskets than it had sold in March. In terms of y, how many gift baskets did Carla's Candy Shop sell in April?

    (A) $y + 5$
    (B) $y - 5$
    (C) $y + 6$
    (D) $y - 6$
    (E) $y + 16$

---

3. If $320 + w = 310$, then what is the value of $10 - w$?

    (A) 0
    (B) 10
    (C) 20
    (D) 300
    (E) 320

CONTINUE TO THE NEXT PAGE

4. Which subtraction problem is equivalent to $\dfrac{2}{5} - \dfrac{1}{3}$?

    (A) $\dfrac{2}{3} - \dfrac{1}{5}$

    (B) $\dfrac{2}{8} - \dfrac{1}{8}$

    (C) $\dfrac{3}{15} - \dfrac{1}{15}$

    (D) $\dfrac{3}{15} - \dfrac{5}{15}$

    (E) $\dfrac{6}{15} - \dfrac{5}{15}$

5. Dwight has three times as many marbles as Erica. If together they have a total of 24 marbles, then how many marbles does Dwight have?

    (A) 6
    (B) 8
    (C) 16
    (D) 18
    (E) 72

6. What is the value of $\dfrac{1}{2} + \dfrac{3}{4} + \dfrac{5}{6}$?

    (A) $\dfrac{9}{12}$

    (B) $1\dfrac{1}{2}$

    (C) $2\dfrac{1}{12}$

    (D) $3\dfrac{5}{12}$

    (E) $3\dfrac{3}{4}$

CONTINUE TO THE NEXT PAGE

7.   When the number *m* is divided by 4, the result is 5 with a remainder of 3. What is the value of *m*?

(A)   20
(B)   23
(C)   25
(D)   27
(E)   30

8.   Which is the value of 5.3 − 1.7 + 4.7?

(A)   −1.1
(B)   8.3
(C)   9.7
(D)   10.4
(E)   11.7

9.   The circumference of a circle is 10π cm. What is the radius of the circle?
($C = 2\pi r$)

(A)   2 cm
(B)   3 cm
(C)   4 cm
(D)   5 cm
(E)   10 cm

10.   If Marlene has 23 trading cards and Lillian has 9 trading cards, how many cards must Marlene give to Lillian in order for them to have the same number of trading cards?

(A)   7
(B)   8
(C)   9
(D)   14
(E)   16

CONTINUE TO THE NEXT PAGE

Questions 11-12 are based on the graph.

The bar graph shows the number of flights delayed at a particular airport for five days.

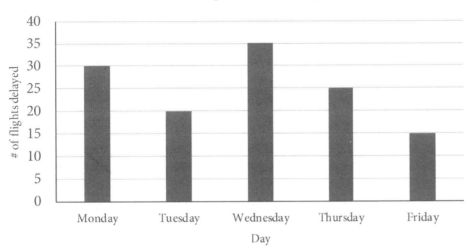

Number of flights delayed by day

11. How many more flights were delayed on the day with the most delayed flights compared to the day with the least delayed flights?

   (A)   3
   (B)   4
   (C)   10
   (D)   15
   (E)   20

12. Which day had 50% fewer delayed flights than Monday?

   (A)   Tuesday
   (B)   Wednesday
   (C)   Thursday
   (D)   Friday
   (E)   No day had 50% fewer delayed flights than Monday

CONTINUE TO THE NEXT PAGE

13. Which expression shows the result when the distributive property is applied to $3(b - 4 + 5b)$?

(A) $3b - 4 + 5b$
(B) $3b - 12 + 15b$
(C) $3b - 12 + 5b$
(D) $3b + 12 - 15b$
(E) $3b + 12 - 5b$

14. The figure shown was created by joining a square and four isosceles right triangles. What is the area, in square units, of the figure?

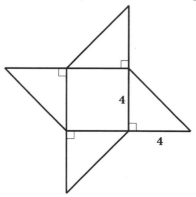

(A) 16
(B) 32
(C) 48
(D) 64
(E) 80

15. What is the result of $\dfrac{1}{4}\left(\dfrac{2}{3} + 4\right)$?

(A) $\dfrac{1}{12}$

(B) $\dfrac{1}{6}$

(C) $\dfrac{7}{6}$

(D) $\dfrac{3}{2}$

(E) $\dfrac{7}{3}$

CONTINUE TO THE NEXT PAGE

16. What is the value of *d* in the equation $2(d - 4) = 24$?

    (A) 10
    (B) 14
    (C) 16
    (D) 20
    (E) 52

17. Irving makes a juice cocktail that has 4 oz. apple juice, 6 oz. of cranberry juice, and 5 oz. of tomato juice. What percent of the juice cocktail is cranberry juice?

    (A) 40%
    (B) 45%
    (C) 50%
    (D) 60%
    (E) 72%

18. Each year, a tree grows a new ring. Four trees currently have a total of 34 rings. How many total rings will those four trees have three years from now?

    (A) 46
    (B) 40
    (C) 38
    (D) 37
    (E) 31

19. In order to make a drink, Rodney uses 4 ounces of coffee for every 6 ounces of milk and 2 ounces of sugar. If he wants to makes 42 ounces of this drink, how many ounces of milk should he use?

    (A) 6
    (B) 7
    (C) 12
    (D) 14
    (E) 21

CONTINUE TO THE NEXT PAGE

20. Luz is putting beads on a string in the order one green, two red, three blue, two black, and then repeating the same pattern again starting with one green bead. If there are exactly 10 blue beads on the string, how many total beads are on the string?

(A) 10
(B) 24
(C) 28
(D) 30
(E) 32

---

21. In the triangle shown, what is the value of $x + 2y$?

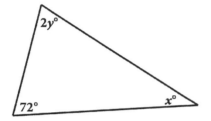

(A) 8
(B) 36
(C) 72
(D) 108
(E) 288

---

22. Rosenda is mixing paint in a container. She has to add 240 milliliters of yellow paint, 320 milliliters of red paint, and then fill the container to the 2 liter mark with water. How much water will she need to add to complete the paint mixture, in milliliters?

(1,000 milliliters = 1 liter)

(A) 440
(B) 560
(C) 1,440
(D) 1,540
(E) 1,560

CONTINUE TO THE NEXT PAGE

23. Patrick wants to make many batches of a recipe that requires four tablespoons of milk per batch. If he has exactly half a gallon of milk, how many batches of this recipe can Patrick make? (1 gallon = 16 cups, 1 cup = 16 tablespoons)

   (A)   24
   (B)   32
   (C)   48
   (D)   64
   (E)   128

24. One train leaves a station and travels south for 6 miles. Another train leaves the same station and travels west for 8 miles. What is the shortest distance between the two trains?

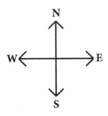

   (A)   10 miles
   (B)   12 miles
   (C)   13 miles
   (D)   14 miles
   (E)   15 miles

25. Regan has taken four tests and her scores were 88, 92, 93, and 85. She has one more test to take and she wants her mean score on the five tests to be at least 90. What is the minimum score she could receive on the fifth test in order to achieve a mean score of at least 90 on all five tests?

   (A)   90
   (B)   92
   (C)   94
   (D)   95
   (E)   96

STOP

Section 2: Reading Comprehension

40 questions
40 minutes

Directions: Read each passage in this section carefully and answer the questions that follow. Choose the best answer based on the passage.

Submersibles are underwater crafts that enable humans to explore the world beneath the surface of large bodies of water. A submersible is similar to a submarine, in that it can travel to great depths and provide protection for its crew. However, unlike submarines, which travel independently, submersibles are connected by a cable to a support ship on the surface of the water. Submersibles are smaller than submarines, but they can travel to greater depths, as long as they remain tethered to the support ship.

Line 5

The first submersible was constructed in 1620 by Cornelius Drebbel. Drebbel's craft was able to dive to depths of up to 15 feet below the surface of the water. It was propelled by wooden oars, rowed by a crew onboard. The crew received fresh air via snorkel air tubes that were kept on top of the water with floats.

10

As one might expect, undersea travel technology has evolved significantly in the 400 years since Drebbel's experimental craft. In 1960, the submersible *Trieste*, carrying a crew of two, dove to over 35,000 feet beneath the ocean's surface. The submersible reached the deepest known part of the ocean, an area near the Mariana Trench in the Pacific Ocean. Like its ancestor, the *Trieste* was connected to a ship on the surface, but it maintained its own air supply and was propelled with a gasoline engine, rather than wooden oars.

15

Oceanographers continue to use submersibles to explore the ocean's depths. Using this technology, they are able to explore deep-water ecosystems and make fascinating observations about the organisms living in these unique environments.

1. From the passage, one can infer that
   (A) both submersibles and submarines are usually self-propelled
   (B) submersibles and submarines have different advantages
   (C) all submersibles get their air from the surface
   (D) submarines were invented before submersibles
   (E) neither submarines nor submersibles are self-propelled

2. As used in line 9, a "snorkel" is most likely
   (A) a system of floats that is attached to a submersible
   (B) a tube that goes above water to carry fresh air underwater
   (C) a way to propel a submersible
   (D) an early kind of submersible
   (E) an invention from the 1600s that can travel underwater

3. The passage shows that submersible technology has progressed over 400 years. "Progressed" most nearly means
   (A) became more expensive
   (B) involved larger engines
   (C) improved
   (D) became more famous
   (E) remained the same

4. It can be inferred that a support ship is
   (A) a ship that can travel above or below water
   (B) an early type of submersible
   (C) a ship on the surface connected to a submersible
   (D) the ship that provides air and fuel to a submersible
   (E) a type of submersible that is self-propelled

5. According to the passage, the *Trieste*
   (A) can hold larger crews than the first submersible
   (B) does not require a support ship
   (C) is propelled by oars
   (D) can dive to much deeper depths than early submersibles
   (E) relies on fresh air delivered by the support ship

CONTINUE TO THE NEXT PAGE

> *This passage is excerpted from Journey to the Center of the Earth by Jules Verne.*
>
> To describe my despair would be impossible. No words could tell it. I was buried alive, with the prospect before me of dying of hunger and thirst. Mechanically I swept the ground with my hands. How dry and hard the rock seemed to me! But how had I left the course of the stream? For it was a terrible fact that it no longer ran at my side. Then I understood the reason of that fearful, silence,
> Line 5 when for the last time I listened to hear if any sound from my companions could reach my ears. At the moment when I left the right road, I had not noticed the absence of the stream. It is evident that at that moment a deviation had presented itself before me, whilst the Hansbach [the stream], following the caprice of another incline, had gone with my companions away into unknown depths. How was I to return? There was not a trace of their footsteps or of my own, for the foot left no
> 10 mark upon the granite floor. I racked my brain for a solution of this impracticable problem. One word described my position. Lost! Lost at an immeasurable depth! Thirty leagues of rock seemed to weigh upon my shoulders with a dreadful pressure. I felt crushed. I tried to carry back my ideas to things on the surface of the earth. I could scarcely succeed. Hamburg, the house in the Königstrasse, my poor Gräuben, all that busy world underneath which I was wandering about, was
> 15 passing in rapid confusion before my terrified memory. I could revive with vivid reality all the incidents of our voyage, Iceland, M. Fridrikssen, Snæfell. I said to myself that if, in such a position as I was now in, I was fool enough to cling to one glimpse of hope, it would be madness, and that the best thing I could do was to despair.

6. From the passage it can be inferred that the narrator

   (A) was following a stream at some point
   (B) wished he'd never come on the trip
   (C) was having a bad dream
   (D) was blind
   (E) was not alone

7. According to the passage, Hansbach is

   (A) the guide on their trip
   (B) the name of a volcano
   (C) the name of a body of water
   (D) the town that the narrator comes from
   (E) the name of the narrator's uncle

8. When the narrator says, "I felt crushed" (line 12), this statement can be interpreted to mean

   (A) the pressure of the rocks above is pressing down on him
   (B) he is laying close to the granite floor of the path
   (C) he is very upset that he is lost
   (D) he is very upset that his companions have left him behind
   (E) he is disappointed by the trip so far

9. What does the narrator hope to find on the ground beneath him?

   (A) a path to the surface
   (B) his own footprints or those of his traveling companions
   (C) water from a nearby stream
   (D) something to eat
   (E) a message from those on the surface

10. The tone of this passage is

   (A) calm
   (B) angry
   (C) disappointed
   (D) curious
   (E) fearful

CONTINUE TO THE NEXT PAGE

On May 20, 2013, a tornado touched down in Newcastle, OK. With winds of up to 210 miles per hour, it was a major tornado. The damage caused in the area was extensive and there were several deaths reported. This weather event was noted for more than its mass destruction, however. Prior to this storm the usual warning time for tornadoes had been 10 to 13 minutes. On May 20,

Line 5   the U.S. Storm Prediction Center was able to provide 16 minutes warning. While that may not seem like a significant increase, very often a few extra minutes can mean the difference between life and death for those in the path of a storm. Those extra minutes in warning time were an important milestone in storm predictions.

         According to meteorologists, the challenge with predicting tornadoes is that there is an element

10   of chance in their formation. Tornadoes are caused by the conflicting rotations of warm and cold air masses. Sometimes these conflicts result in thunderstorms or hail, but other times, when a downdraft develops, a tornado forms. Even when the atmospheric factors align for a tornado, the chances of a tornado hitting the ground are small. Thanks to improved high-speed computer technology that can analyze data faster, scientists can now more accurately and quickly assess when

15   a storm will touch down. As tornado predictions improve, it also becomes easier to get residents to heed the warnings. In the past, warnings were frequently issued, but when no tornado emerged, many people would ignore serious threats. Greater accuracy can only help with this problem.

11. Which could be reasonably concluded from this passage?

   (A) Hail usually precedes a tornado.
   (B) Tornadoes always occur when conflicting air masses meet.
   (C) A downdraft, combined with other weather elements, can cause a tornado.
   (D) Tornadoes are caused by thunderstorms.
   (E) Tornadoes occur when there is rain, hail, or thunder and lightning.

12. Based on this passage, a "milestone" (line 8) is

   (A) a large hail stone that accompanies tornadoes
   (B) an extremely powerful weather event
   (C) an event that marks an important change
   (D) a way to alert people of tornadoes
   (E) a weather pattern associated with tornadoes

13. According to the passage, why is it challenging to predict tornadoes?

   (A) Similar weather conditions may or may not produce a tornado.
   (B) It is difficult to track fast moving warm and cold air patterns.
   (C) The downdraft is not detectable.
   (D) Tornadoes are infrequent.
   (E) It is difficult to observe tornadoes when so little warning is given before they strike.

14. Which statement best captures the main idea of this passage?

   (A) The 2013 tornado in Newcastle, OK, was very powerful.
   (B) Scientists don't believe they will ever be able to provide more than a few minutes of advance warning before tornadoes occur.
   (C) Scientists have never provided more than 15 minutes warning of an oncoming tornado.
   (D) The ability to predict tornadoes has improved over the years because of advances in computer technology.
   (E) Many powerful tornadoes have struck throughout Oklahoma.

15. Based on this passage, it can be inferred that

   (A) scientists enjoy studying tornadoes
   (B) tornadoes can be deadly
   (C) tornadoes rarely occur
   (D) more tornadoes hit Oklahoma than any other state
   (E) scientists don't know what causes a tornado

CONTINUE TO THE NEXT PAGE

The following passage is excerpted from The Secret Garden by Frances Hodgson Burnett.

The sun shone down for nearly a week on the secret garden. The Secret Garden was what Mary called it when she was thinking of it. She liked the name, and she liked still more the feeling that when its beautiful old walls shut her in no one knew where she was. It seemed almost like being shut out of the world in some fairy place. The few books she had read and liked had been fairy-
Line 5 story books, and she had read of secret gardens in some of the stories. Sometimes people went to sleep in them for a hundred years, which she had thought must be rather stupid. She had no intention of going to sleep, and, in fact, she was becoming wider awake every day which passed. She was beginning to like to be out of doors; she no longer hated the wind, but enjoyed it. She could run faster, and longer, and she could skip up to a hundred. The bulbs in the secret garden
_10_ must have been much astonished. Such nice clear places were made round them that they had all the breathing space they wanted, and really, if Mistress Mary had known it, they began to cheer up under the dark earth and work tremendously. The sun could get at them and warm them, and when the rain came down it could reach them at once, so they began to feel very much alive.

Mary was an odd, determined little person, and now she had something interesting to be
_15_ determined about, she was very much absorbed, indeed. She worked and dug and pulled up weeds steadily, only becoming more pleased with her work every hour instead of tiring of it. It seemed to her like a fascinating sort of play. She found many more of the sprouting pale green points than she had ever hoped to find. They seemed to be starting up everywhere and each day she was sure she found tiny new ones, some so tiny that they barely peeped above the earth.

16. According to the passage, what change has come over Mary because of the Secret Garden?

(A) She enjoys being outside more.
(B) She is more interested in reading.
(C) She feels alone and cut off from the world.
(D) She is more interested in how plants grow.
(E) She is more thoughtful than she was before.

17. Which of the following is an example of personification in this passage?

(A) Mary
(B) the wind
(C) the dark earth
(D) the bulbs growing in the ground
(E) the sun

18. According to the passage, Mary refers to this place as the "Secret Garden" because

(A) no one else knows it exists
(B) she does not tell anyone she that visits it
(C) the plants and flowers are hidden away
(D) she feels much more alive when she is there
(E) she has read about secret gardens in stories

19. From the passage it can be inferred that "bulbs" (line 9) are

(A) clear glass ornaments decorating the garden
(B) seeds of flowers growing underground
(C) the light from the sun that falls behind the wall
(D) the reason why Mary calls this place the secret garden
(E) a reflection of the clouds in the sky

20. What effect do Mary's activities have on the plants growing in the garden?

(A) The plants are being trampled beneath her feet.
(B) The plants are growing more slowly.
(C) The plants are responding to her reading from the fairy stories.
(D) She waters them on dry days, which is waking them up.
(E) Mary is clearing away the weeds, giving the plants clear spaces to in which to grow.

CONTINUE TO THE NEXT PAGE

Mount Everest, located in Asia between Tibet and Nepal, spans 29,000 feet above sea level and is the highest mountain on Earth. English surveyors in the 1850s were the first to scientifically measure the height of the peak. These surveyors gave the mountain the name Everest. The mountain is also known as Sagarmatha to the people who have lived there for centuries.

Line 5   The Sherpa tribe has been living in the Himalayan range for generations. Their physiology is uniquely adapted to the atmospheric conditions of this high altitude area, where there is a lower proportion of oxygen in the air. The Sherpas have lived at high altitudes for so long that their bodies are much more efficient at using the oxygen available, allowing them to function at altitudes that could be deadly to climbers accustomed to living at lower altitudes.

10   Almost every westerner who has ever explored the great mountain was only able to do so with the help of local climbers from the Sherpa tribe. In 1953, the achievement of the first successful climb to the summit was shared by New Zealander Edmund Hillary (a British subject) and Tenzing Norgay, a local Sherpa. While Hillary enjoyed widespread media attention and was honored by the Queen of England, the honors bestowed upon Norgay were fewer and less publicized. Nevertheless,

15   Norgay always insisted that he felt he had been acknowledged adequately. His son, however, disagreed. In his 2001 book, *Touching My Father's Soul: A Sherpa's Journey to the top of Everest*, Jamling Norgay argued that the Sherpas risk their lives guiding climbers, but receive none of the accolades when they succeed and little notice when they die on the mountain.

21. In line 14, the phrase "bestowed upon" most nearly means

(A) given to
(B) ignored
(C) donated to
(D) refused
(E) denied to

22. Based on information in the passage, which is the most accurate description of a "Sherpa"?

(A) a type of specialized climbing equipment
(B) a surveyor who determined the height of Mount Everest
(C) a book written by Jamling Norgay
(D) a member of a tribe of people who live near Mount Everest
(E) an explorer from New Zealand

23. What can be reasonably inferred from this passage?

(A) Sherpas have died while climbing Everest.
(B) Everest was first spotted by English surveyors.
(C) Everyone who has ever climbed Everest has been European.
(D) The Sherpas resent all Europeans who come to climb the mountain.
(E) There are border disputes between Tibet and Nepal over Mount Everest.

24. Based on the passage, how does Jamling Norgay's opinion of the Sherpas' role differ from his father's?

(A) Tenzing Norgay believed Sherpas had a responsibility to guide people up the mountain, while Jamling disagreed.
(B) Jamling Norgay believed Sherpas should be paid more, but his father did not.
(C) Tenzing Norgay did not feel Sherpas should write about climbing the mountain, but his son, Jamling, decided to publish a book.
(D) Tenzing believed he was acknowledged for the first climb, while his son did not believe Sherpas received the credit they deserved.
(E) Jamling Norgay worried that many Sherpas die climbing Everest, but his father believed the risks and sacrifices were warranted.

25. What is the main idea of this passage?

(A) Members of the Sherpa tribe have played an important, but sometimes unacknowledged, role in the exploration of Mount Everest.
(B) Jamling Norgay believes his father was exploited by Edmund Hillary and others.
(C) The media has discriminated against Sherpas.
(D) The real honors related to exploring and climbing Mount Everest belong to the Sherpas.
(E) The work of Sherpas on Everest is dangerous.

CONTINUE TO THE NEXT PAGE

This passage is excerpted from Uncle Tom's Cabin *by Harriet Beecher Stowe.*

"O, Mr. Shelby…how can I ever hold up my head again among them, if, for the sake of a little paltry gain, we sell such a faithful, excellent, confiding creature as poor Tom? I have talked with Eliza about her boy—her duty to him as a Christian mother… I have told her that one soul is worth more than all the money in the world; and how will she believe me when she sees us turn
Line 5   round and sell her child?—sell him, perhaps, to certain ruin of body and soul!"

"I'm sorry you feel so about it,—indeed I am," said Mr. Shelby; "and I respect your feelings, too, though I don't pretend to share them to their full extent; but I tell you now, solemnly, it's of no use—I can't help myself. I didn't mean to tell you this Emily; but, in plain words, there is no choice between selling these two and selling everything. Either they must go, or all must. Haley has come
10   into possession of a mortgage, which, if I don't clear off with him directly, will take everything. I've raked, and scraped, and borrowed, and all but begged,—and the price of these two was needed to make up the balance, and I had to give them up. Haley fancied the child; he agreed to settle the matter that way, and no other. I was in his power, and had to do it. If you feel so to have them sold, would it be any better to have all sold?

26. It can be inferred that Eliza is

    (A) Mr. Shelby's wife
    (B) Mr. Haley's wife
    (C) a woman who is a slave and is being sold
    (D) a woman who disagrees with Mr. Shelby's decision
    (E) Tom's mother

27. As used in line 2, the word "paltry" is closest in meaning to

    (A) plenty
    (B) valuable
    (C) disgraceful
    (D) worthy
    (E) insignificant

28. Why is Emily upset about the sale of Tom?

    (A) She is very fond of Tom.
    (B) She is worried about what they will do without their slaves.
    (C) She is afraid of what the other slaves will do.
    (D) She is angry that Mr. Shelby did not discuss the problem with her.
    (E) She has stressed to Tom's mother that a human soul cannot be bought and sold.

29. Based on information in the passage, how does Mr. Shelby feel about the sale of Tom?

    (A) He doesn't want to do it, but feels he has no choice.
    (B) He has long considered the selling Tom without regret.
    (C) He doesn't understand why his wife is so upset.
    (D) He wants to sell Tom and another slave as soon as possible and put it behind him.
    (E) He doesn't believe in slavery, but he has to earn a living.

30. What will happen if Mr. Shelby doesn't sell Tom?

    (A) He will have to ask Mr. Haley to buy a different slave.
    (B) Mr. Haley will leave town and be angry.
    (C) Tom will likely leave on his own.
    (D) Mrs. Shelby will be angry with him.
    (E) Mr. Shelby will lose everything else he owns.

CONTINUE TO THE NEXT PAGE

This passage is excerpted from "Song of Wandering Aengus" by William Butler Yeats.

I went out to the hazel wood,
Because a fire was in my head,
And cut and peeled a hazel wand,
And hooked a berry to a thread;
Line 5   And when white moths were on the wing,
And moth-like stars were flickering out,
I dropped the berry in a stream
And caught a little silver trout.

10   When I had laid it on the floor
I went to blow the fire a-flame,
But something rustled on the floor,
And someone called me by my name:
It had become a glimmering girl
15   With apple blossom in her hair
Who called me by my name and ran
And faded through the brightening air.

Though I am old with wandering
20   Through hollow lands and hilly lands,
I will find out where she has gone,
And kiss her lips and take her hands;
And walk among long dappled grass,
And pluck till time and times are done,
25   The silver apples of the moon,
The golden apples of the sun.

31. In this poem, what are the moon and the sun compared to?

    (A) blossoms
    (B) apples
    (C) a beautiful girl
    (D) a trout
    (E) the life of an old man

32. It can be inferred from the poem that a "hazel" is most likely

    (A) a type of tree
    (B) the name of a woman
    (C) a type of berry
    (D) a type of cloth
    (E) a type of fish

33. According to the poem, what is transformed into a beautiful girl?

    (A) a moth
    (B) an apple blossom
    (C) a hazel wand
    (D) a trout
    (E) an apple

34. What is the main idea of the last stanza?

    (A) The speaker is an old man but is still determined to find the girl.
    (B) Now that he is older, the speaker realizes he imagined the girl.
    (C) The speaker is too tired to search for the girl.
    (D) The speaker wasted his life looking for the girl.
    (E) The girl is hiding from the speaker, and he must continue to find clues to locate her.

CONTINUE TO THE NEXT PAGE

35. The speaker wants to find the girl in order to

   (A) prove that she was not imaginary
   (B) live the rest of his life with her
   (C) recapture his own youth
   (D) ask her why she left
   (E) follow the patterns of the moon

Line 5

10

15

     In the 1400s, people who lived in Europe were desperate to obtain spices. At the time, spices were used for preserving food and preventing spoilage. The problem was that many of these spices came from Asia. Travel over land between Europe and Asia was dangerous and expensive. The Silk Road, or the road that ran between Europe and Asia, was frequently not usable due to wars and an unforgiving climate. In order to fulfill their subjects' desire for spices, many European rulers began to sponsor exploration trips to find a sea route from Europe to various parts of Asia. Thus began the Age of Exploration.
     The first country to begin sponsoring explorers was Portugal. Prince Henry of Portugal sent crews that found a route to the west coast of Africa. In order to reach Asia, however, sailors had to sail around the Cape of Good Hope at the southern tip of Africa and through the Indian Ocean. Portuguese explorer Vasco de Gama achieved this remarkable feat, and Portugal established dominance in the India-Europe trade routes. When Christopher Columbus requested funding to explore a new route to Asia, however, the rulers of Portugal refused. Spain, then, financed the trip instead and thus laid claim to much of the continent that Christopher Columbus actually landed on: North America.

---

36. Which title best summarizes the main idea of this passage?

   (A) European Explorers Throughout History
   (B) Vasco de Gama: Discoverer of North America
   (C) A Hunger for Spices Led to World Exploration
   (D) Spices: The Untold Story
   (E) Christopher Columbus' Great Accomplishment

37. The author most likely includes information about the Silk Road in order to

   (A) prove the popularity of spices
   (B) explain why it was important to find a sea route from Europe to Asia
   (C) describe where spices were traded
   (D) emphasize the instability of the 1400s
   (E) provide evidence for the primary argument

38. The tone of this passage can best be described as

   (A) informative
   (B) persuasive
   (C) ironic
   (D) wistful
   (E) sarcastic

39. Based on information in the passage, all of the following statements are true EXCEPT

   (A) Prince Henry of Portugal did not finance Christopher Columbus's exploration of a new route to Asia
   (B) spices were not widely produced in Europe in the 1400s
   (C) the sea route from Europe to Asia was preferred over the land route
   (D) Christopher Columbus found a route to North America, not Asia as he intended
   (E) the best known explorers from the Age of Exploration were all Portugese

40. This passage would most likely be found in

   (A) an almanac
   (B) an explorer's autobiography
   (C) a newspaper article
   (D) a history textbook
   (E) a persuasive essay

STOP

Section 3: Verbal

60 questions
30 minutes

This section has two types of questions – synonyms and analogies.

Synonyms

Directions: Each question has a word in all capital letters and then five answer choices that are in lower case letters. Choose the answer choice that has the word (or phrase) that is closest in meaning to the word that is in capital letters.

1. DAMAGE:

    (A) abandon
    (B) weaken
    (C) sacrifice
    (D) sort
    (E) disturb

2. TENDER:

    (A) quiet
    (B) thrilling
    (C) compact
    (D) dreadful
    (E) sore

3. PERSIST:

    (A) continue
    (B) take
    (C) reassure
    (D) rely
    (E) manage

4. WILLINGLY:

    (A) permanently
    (B) reasonably
    (C) earnestly
    (D) voluntarily
    (E) fully

5. PLAIN:

    (A) strained
    (B) dainty
    (C) simple
    (D) meek
    (E) costly

6. CHARACTERISTIC:

    (A) stopped
    (B) large
    (C) startled
    (D) hollow
    (E) typical

CONTINUE TO THE NEXT PAGE

7. SUBMIT:

    (A) trespass
    (B) surrender
    (C) preview
    (D) scurry
    (E) dread

8. VENUE:

    (A) location
    (B) logistics
    (C) guidance
    (D) division
    (E) report

9. DEVIATE:

    (A) register
    (B) exaggerate
    (C) stray
    (D) pose
    (E) clatter

10. FLAUNT:

    (A) transform
    (B) soak
    (C) rise
    (D) parade
    (E) illustrate

11. RADIANT:

    (A) demanding
    (B) eager
    (C) still
    (D) thirsty
    (E) glowing

12. IRK:

    (A) bother
    (B) dash
    (C) shake
    (D) measure
    (E) creak

13. TEMPERATE:

    (A) classic
    (B) mild
    (C) intangible
    (D) fond
    (E) prosperous

14. IMPART:

    (A) inspect
    (B) mail
    (C) inform
    (D) fear
    (E) mimic

15. DISTORT:

    (A) purchase
    (B) fade
    (C) improvise
    (D) twist
    (E) burden

16. CANDID:

    (A) temporary
    (B) honest
    (C) aggressive
    (D) jovial
    (E) forgettable

17. MALICIOUS:

    (A) nasty
    (B) careful
    (C) unhappy
    (D) impulsive
    (E) faint

18. TRIVIAL:

    (A) misplaced
    (B) definite
    (C) familiar
    (D) incompetent
    (E) unimportant

CONTINUE TO THE NEXT PAGE

19. IDIOM:

   (A) victory
   (B) expression
   (C) appearance
   (D) emotion
   (E) wound

20. LIVID:

   (A) timorous
   (B) respectful
   (C) angry
   (D) beneficial
   (E) silent

21. OBJECTIVE:

   (A) meager
   (B) limp
   (C) adverse
   (D) neutral
   (E) generous

22. PRECARIOUS:

   (A) insecure
   (B) familiar
   (C) dismayed
   (D) lost
   (E) terrible

23. RESERVED:

   (A) customary
   (B) quiet
   (C) thriving
   (D) embarassed
   (E) bulging

24. ADMONISH:

   (A) prescribe
   (B) rest
   (C) exclude
   (D) cultivate
   (E) warn

25. EPHEMERAL:

   (A) appearing unexpectedly
   (B) moving slowly
   (C) dissappearing quickly
   (D) walking silently
   (E) planning carefully

26. SEDATE:

   (A) absolute
   (B) efficient
   (C) safe
   (D) calm
   (E) rehearsed

27. SLY:

   (A) without confidence
   (B) not trustworthy
   (C) quickly advancing
   (D) lacking authority
   (E) very unsure

28. DILUTE:

   (A) weaken
   (B) gloat
   (C) tarnish
   (D) blame
   (E) measure

29. SCRUPLE:

   (A) legend
   (B) waste
   (C) fuss
   (D) talent
   (E) moral

30. PRECOCIOUS:

   (A) judicial
   (B) advanced
   (C) unique
   (D) satisfactory
   (E) fickle

CONTINUE TO THE NEXT PAGE

Analogies

Directions: Identify the relationships between the words. Then choose the answer choice that best finishes the sentence.

31. Retreat is to progress as present is to

    (A) show
    (B) fade
    (C) exclaim
    (D) move
    (E) hide

32. Paddle is to canoe as

    (A) propeller is to airplane
    (B) suitcase is to baggage
    (C) bicycle is to pedal
    (D) buckle is to belt
    (E) faucet is to tap

33. Culprit is to crime as

    (A) visitor is to map
    (B) hero is to rescue
    (C) correspondent is to journal
    (D) subway is to transit
    (E) protégé is to lessons

34. Plum is to prune as

    (A) tree is to apple
    (B) raisin is to grape
    (C) hammock is to bed
    (D) mud is to dirt
    (E) morsel is to chunk

35. Horse is to stampede as bee is to

    (A) bull
    (B) kindred
    (C) swarm
    (D) sea
    (E) goose

36. Rose is to thorn as

    (A) carnation is to stem
    (B) skunk is to spray
    (C) cloth is to rag
    (D) pumpkin is to gourd
    (E) shrub is to grass

37. Request is to require as

    (A) donate is to give
    (B) might is to may
    (C) must is to could
    (D) probably is to doubtfully
    (E) ask is to demand

38. Ripple is to splash as

    (A) wade is to swim
    (B) mingle is to mix
    (C) chew is to taste
    (D) litter is to collect
    (E) question is to solve

39. Thunder is to boom as

    (A) lightning is to storm
    (B) earthquake is to rumble
    (C) rain is to hurricane
    (D) tornado is to funnel
    (E) drought is to water

40. Puppy is to dog as

    (A) kid is to goat
    (B) shark is to fish
    (C) cat is to kitten
    (D) lion is to jungle
    (E) cow is to bull

CONTINUE TO THE NEXT PAGE

41. Flicker is to light as

(A) subscribe is to magazine
(B) fetch is to ball
(C) economical is to stun
(D) tremble is to muscle
(E) dredge is to river

42. Abundant is to harvest as

(A) ragged is to sheets
(B) crowded is to theater
(C) sullied is to reputation
(D) relaxed is to machinery
(E) dazzling is to city

43. Pillar is to support as

(A) wall is to leaning
(B) porch is to entering
(C) adhesive is to join
(D) function is to tool
(E) illusion is to clarify

44. Crease is to fold as

(A) bruise is to collision
(B) mound is to hill
(C) seal is to jar
(D) level is to floor
(E) clutter is to mess

45. Trees is to orchard as grass is to

(A) spring
(B) wheat
(C) sunshine
(D) mower
(E) field

46. Affection is to love as

(A) friendship is to hostility
(B) grace is to dancer
(C) dissatisfaction is to loathing
(D) reputation is to trust
(E) fortune is to luck

47. Merchant is to store as officer is to

(A) station
(B) motorcycle
(C) uniform
(D) patrol
(E) canine

48. Practical is to fanciful as

(A) restless is to agitated
(B) shallow is to deep
(C) bulging is to curved
(D) wise is to informed
(E) plain is to lazy

49. Flawless is to defect as random is to

(A) equality
(B) fright
(C) sacrifice
(D) pattern
(E) dread

50. Diner is to restaurant as

(A) breakfast is to lunch
(B) plate is to tablecloth
(C) knob is to door
(D) paint is to wall
(E) jeans is to pants

51. Revolve is to turn as

(A) discard is to reject
(B) sag is to leak
(C) enroll is to allow
(D) grasp is to release
(E) witness is to ignore

52. Hush is to quiet as

(A) furnish is to warm
(B) stack is to jumbled
(C) encourage is to inspired
(D) forgive is to sorry
(E) record is to lost

CONTINUE TO THE NEXT PAGE

53. Album is to pictures as

   (A) tablet is to stone
   (B) chest is to blankets
   (C) mold is to shape
   (D) sack is to burlap
   (E) bale is to hay

54. Smelly is to putrid as

   (A) ridiculous is to foolish
   (B) creaky is to decrepit
   (C) embarassed is to pleased
   (D) natural is to slender
   (E) humorous is to dull

55. Engineer is to drawings as

   (A) writer is to manuscript
   (B) carpenter is to nails
   (C) astronomer is to stars
   (D) composer is to piano
   (E) scientist is to experiments

56. Twig is to branch as

   (A) chord is to string
   (B) verse is to song
   (C) thicket is to bush
   (D) roll is to loaf
   (E) stew is to soup

57. Survey is to questions as

   (A) advertisement is to sales
   (B) reward is to prize
   (C) guard is to security
   (D) weeds is to dandelions
   (E) compound is to buildings

58. Curtain is to window as

   (A) brush is to hair
   (B) stamp is to ink
   (C) paste is to glue
   (D) lid is to pot
   (E) crumb is to food

59. Bounty is to plentiful as

   (A) outrage is to soothing
   (B) luxury is to extravagant
   (C) feature is to essential
   (D) sickness is to virus
   (E) opportunity is to lively

60. Propaganda is to convince as

   (A) damage is to destroy
   (B) arrangement is to solve
   (C) etiquette is to respect
   (D) reservation is to retreat
   (E) permission is to obey

STOP

Section 4: Quantitative

25 questions
30 minutes

Directions: Each problem is followed by five answer choices. Solve each problem and then decide which answer choice is best.

---

1. In the number 4,312.0$\underline{8}$7, what is the value of the underlined digit?

   (A) eight hundred
   (B) eighty
   (C) eight
   (D) eight-hundredths
   (E) eight-thousandths

---

2. There are 20 students in Mr. Copeland's class. If 8 of these students bought lunch on a particular day, what percent of students did NOT buy lunch on that day?

   (A) 40%
   (B) 60%
   (C) 62%
   (D) 65%
   (E) 70%

---

3. What is the value of $\frac{2}{3} \div \frac{1}{3}$?

   (A) 2
   (B) 1
   (C) $\frac{2}{3}$
   (D) $\frac{1}{3}$
   (E) $\frac{2}{9}$

CONTINUE TO THE NEXT PAGE

4.   Which shows this shape after it is reflected over the dashed line?

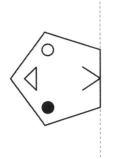

(A)

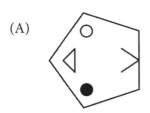

(B)

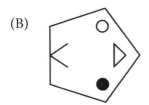

(C)

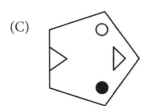

(D)

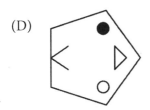

(E)

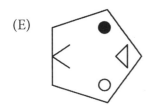

CONTINUE TO THE NEXT PAGE

5. June spent $3.85 on lunch each day for five days. Approximately what was the total that June spent on lunch on those five days?

    (A) $4
    (B) $8
    (C) $12
    (D) $15
    (E) $20

6. The circle graph shows the results of a survey of 200 students who were each asked to identify their favorite subject in school. How many students identified "other" as their favorite subject?

    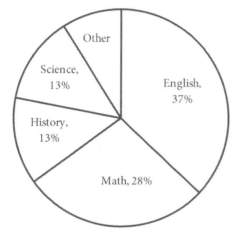

    (A) 4
    (B) 5
    (C) 9
    (D) 18
    (E) 91

CONTINUE TO THE NEXT PAGE

7. A rectangle with a length of 8 cm and a height of 6 cm is divided as shown to create two right triangles. What is the area, in square centimeters, of each triangle?

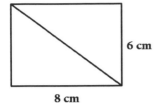

8 cm

6 cm

(A)   14
(B)   24
(C)   28
(D)   32
(E)   48

8. The two triangles shown are similar. What is the value of x?

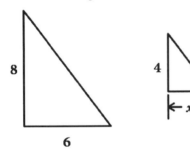

8

6

4

x

(A)   1
(B)   2
(C)   3
(D)   4
(E)   12

9. Meredith took 1 hour and 14 minutes to complete a math test. Brandon completed the same test in 58 minutes. How much longer did it take Meredith to complete the test than Brandon, in minutes?

(A)   9
(B)   12
(C)   14
(D)   16
(E)   56

CONTINUE TO THE NEXT PAGE

10. Darren has m toy trucks in her collection. Delia has $2m - 4$ toy trucks in her collection. How many trucks does Darren have in his collection if Delia has 22 trucks in her collection?

 (A) 4
 (B) 6
 (C) 9
 (D) 13
 (E) 80

11. Which shows the numbers $\frac{2}{3}$, 0.8, 75%, 0.7, and 81% in order from least to greatest?

 (A) 81%, 0.8, 75%, 0.7, $\frac{2}{3}$

 (B) 0.7, 75%, $\frac{2}{3}$, 0.8, 81%

 (C) 0.7, $\frac{2}{3}$, 75%, 0.8, 81%

 (D) $\frac{2}{3}$, 0.7, 75%, 81%, 0.8

 (E) $\frac{2}{3}$, 0.7, 75%, 0.8, 81%

12. What is the greatest common factor of 36 and 54?

 (A) 36
 (B) 18
 (C) 9
 (D) 6
 (E) 3

13. Which expression represents "five less than twice the product of x and y"?

 (A) $5 - 2xy$
 (B) $2xy - 5$
 (C) $5 - 2(x/y)$
 (D) $2(x/y) - 5$
 (E) $5(2) - xy$

CONTINUE TO THE NEXT PAGE

14. Which is the value of 13,792 ÷ 16?

   (A) 792
   (B) 805
   (C) 836
   (D) 837
   (E) 862

15. There are *m* green stickers in a package. If there are 54 stickers in the package, which expression represents how many stickers are not green?

   (A) 54 + *m*
   (B) *m* – 54
   (C) 54 – *m*
   (D) 54*m*
   (E) $\dfrac{m}{54}$

16. If $\dfrac{x}{y} > 1$ and *x* is positive, then which statement must be true?

   (A) *y* must be negative
   (B) *y* must be greater than 1
   (C) the sum of *x* and *y* must be greater than 1
   (D) *x* must be greater than *y* and *y* is positive
   (E) *y* must be greater than *x* and *y* is positive

17. Lydia participated in a triathlon race where she had to run, swim, and then ride a bike. She completed the run portion in 60 minutes. The swim portion of the race took her $\dfrac{2}{3}$ of the time it took her to complete the run portion. The bike portion took her $\dfrac{1}{2}$ of the time it took her to complete the run portion. How long did it take her to complete the total race?

   (A) 1 hour 52 minutes
   (B) 2 hours 5 minutes
   (C) 2 hours 10 minutes
   (D) 2 hours 20 minutes
   (E) 2 hours 25 minutes

CONTINUE TO THE NEXT PAGE

18. In Ms. Norris' class, $\frac{1}{3}$ of the students have at least one sister. Of the students who have at least one sister, $\frac{1}{4}$ also have at least one brother. What fraction of the students have at least one sister and at least one brother?

   (A) $\frac{1}{24}$

   (B) $\frac{1}{12}$

   (C) $\frac{1}{4}$

   (D) $\frac{5}{12}$

   (E) $\frac{7}{12}$

19. Murray is rolling a number cube three times with faces numbered 1-6. What is the probability that the cube will land with the number 4 on the top face of the cube all three times?

   (A) $\frac{1}{216}$

   (B) $\frac{1}{36}$

   (C) $\frac{1}{6}$

   (D) $\frac{1}{3}$

   (E) $\frac{1}{2}$

20. Simplify the expression $5 + 16 \div 4 + 3^2 \times 6$.

   (A) 40
   (B) 48
   (C) 52
   (D) 54
   (E) 63

CONTINUE TO THE NEXT PAGE

21. Three boards are placed overlapping, as shown in the figure below. The two end boards are each 10 feet long and the middle board is 6 feet long. If they overlap by 1 foot where they are connected, what is the overall length, *M*, in feet?

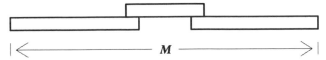

(A)   20
(B)   22
(C)   24
(D)   25
(E)   26

22. A machine produces 300 bolts per hour. How long will it take for this machine to produce 975 bolts?

(A)   3 hours 15 minutes
(B)   3 hours 22 minutes
(C)   3 hours 30 minutes
(D)   3 hours 35 minutes
(E)   3 hours 45 minutes

CONTINUE TO THE NEXT PAGE

23. The coordinate plane below represents a neighborhood and the grid lines are streets. If Antoinette wants to walk from her house to Sherri's house, traveling only along streets, what is the shortest distance she could travel, in units?

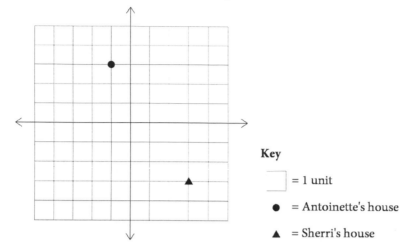

Key

☐ = 1 unit

● = Antoinette's house

▲ = Sherri's house

(A) 4
(B) 5
(C) 8
(D) 10
(E) 11

24. If $\#m\# = m^2 + 2m$, then what is the value of $\#6\#$?

(A) 24
(B) 36
(C) 38
(D) 42
(E) 48

25. What is the surface area, in square centimeters, of a cube that has a side length of 4 cm?

(A) 16
(B) 32
(C) 48
(D) 64
(E) 96

STOP

Practice Test 2

Writing Sample

The writing sample is a way for schools to learn a little more about you. Below are two possible writing topics. Please choose the topic that you find most interesting. Fill in the circle next to the topic you choose and then use this page and the next to write your essay.

(A)   The door slowly opened and…

(B)   I didn't know quite what to think of…

Complete your writing sample on this page and the next. You have 25 minutes to complete this section.

CONTINUE TO THE NEXT PAGE

STOP

Section 1: Quantitative

25 questions
30 minutes

Directions: Each problem is followed by five answer choices. Solve each problem and then decide which answer choice is best.

---

1. The Sims family is going on a car trip that is 1,403 miles long. They are going to spend three days on this trip and want to drive about the same distance each day. Approximately how many miles must they drive each day?

    (A) 3
    (B) 5
    (C) 400
    (D) 500
    (E) 750

---

2. If $290 + \square + \Delta = 356$, then what is the value of $\square + \Delta$?

    (A) 6
    (B) 50
    (C) 56
    (D) 66
    (E) 76

---

3. Whitney bought 4 dozen pencils and divided them equally among her classmates. If each classmate received 3 pencils, how many classmates does Whitney have?

    (A) 8
    (B) 12
    (C) 14
    (D) 15
    (E) 16

CONTINUE TO THE NEXT PAGE

4.   Ricky has 75 cents. He wants to buy erasers that cost 16 cents each. What is the maximum number of erasers that he can buy?

(A)   4
(B)   5
(C)   6
(D)   32
(E)   64

5.   How many edges does this figure have?

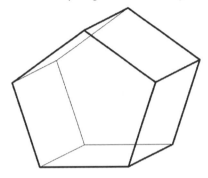

(A)   5
(B)   10
(C)   12
(D)   15
(E)   20

CONTINUE TO THE NEXT PAGE

6. Which of the following shows a figure that is shaded in more than $\frac{1}{2}$ of its area?

(A)

(B)

(C)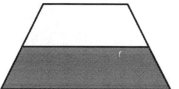

(D)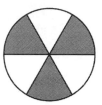

(E)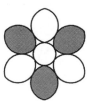

7. Which number has a value that is $\frac{1}{100}$ the value of 304.526?

(A) 0.304526

(B) 3.04526

(C) 30.4526

(D) 3,045.26

(E) 30,452.6

CONTINUE TO THE NEXT PAGE

8. What is the value of $\dfrac{7}{8} \times \dfrac{8}{9} \times \dfrac{9}{10}$?

    (A) $\dfrac{7}{10}$

    (B) $\dfrac{8}{12}$

    (C) $\dfrac{42}{36}$

    (D) $\dfrac{108}{72}$

    (E) $\dfrac{540}{90}$

---

9. Sandra bought a package of candies. She gave 4 candies each to her 21 classmates and had 6 candies left over. How many candies were in the package?

    (A)   78
    (B)   90
    (C)   94
    (D)   95
    (E)   98

---

10. If 30% of a number is 24, then what is 75% of that same number?

    (A)   36
    (B)   48
    (C)   60
    (D)   72
    (E)   84

---

11. Jamar ran a 5 kilometer race. He ran the first 2 kilometers in 14 minutes. If he ran at the same pace for the rest of the race, how many minutes total did it take him to complete the 5 kilometer race?

    (A)   7 minutes
    (B)   21 minutes
    (C)   28 minutes
    (D)   35 minutes
    (E)   42 minutes

CONTINUE TO THE NEXT PAGE

12. Which is the value of $\frac{4}{5}$ divided by $\frac{2}{3}$?

  (A) $\frac{8}{15}$

  (B) $\frac{3}{5}$

  (C) $\frac{2}{3}$

  (D) $\frac{11}{10}$

  (E) $\frac{6}{5}$

13. If 14 is 40% of a number b, then what is the value of b?

  (A) 5.6
  (B) 7
  (C) 28
  (D) 30
  (E) 35

14. What is the volume, in cubic units, of the prism shown?

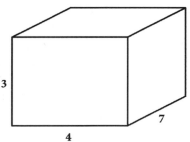

  (A) 14
  (B) 42
  (C) 84
  (D) 96
  (E) 168

CONTINUE TO THE NEXT PAGE

15. A car rental company charges S dollars for the first three days of a rental and T dollars a day after the first three days. Which expression represents the cost, in dollars, of renting a car from them for eight days?

    (A) $S + (8 \times T)$
    (B) $S + (5 \times T)$
    (C) $8 \times (S \times T)$
    (D) $(3 \times S) + (8 \times T)$
    (E) $(3 \times S) + (5 \times T)$

16. If $m - 5 > 14$, then what is the least possible whole number value of m?

    (A) 9
    (B) 10
    (C) 18
    (D) 19
    (E) 20

17. There are 92 students going on a fieldtrip, and they must divide into five groups. If no group has more than one student more than another group, what is the least number of students who could be in a group?

    (A) 1
    (B) 18
    (C) 19
    (D) 20
    (E) 22

18. Lourdes is choosing candies from a bag that has 5 yellow candies, 5 green candies, and 16 blue candies. If she chooses 2 candies from the bag without replacing the first candy, what is the probability she will choose 2 green candies?

    (A) $\dfrac{2}{65}$

    (B) $\dfrac{5}{169}$

    (C) $\dfrac{5}{26}$

    (D) $\dfrac{9}{26}$

    (E) $\dfrac{6}{13}$

CONTINUE TO THE NEXT PAGE

19. If a circle has a diameter of 16 cm, what is the approximate area of that circle, in cm?
    ($A = \pi r^2$ and $\pi \approx 3.14$)

    (A)   16
    (B)   25.12
    (C)   200.96
    (D)   232.48
    (E)   803.84

20. How many inches are in 4 miles? (1 mile = 5,280 feet and 1 foot = 12 inches)

    (A)   440
    (B)   5,280
    (C)   63,360
    (D)   253,440
    (E)   506,880

21. The chart below shows how many dogs visited a park over six days.

Day	Number of dogs
1	12
2	14
3	21
4	16
5	9
6	21

    What was the median number of dogs that visited the park each day?

    (A)   12
    (B)   14
    (C)   15
    (D)   16
    (E)   21

CONTINUE TO THE NEXT PAGE

22. Essie asked 30 people whether they preferred bananas, apples, oranges, or melon. Each person was allowed to choose only one fruit. If $\frac{1}{3}$ of the people chose bananas, 30% chose apples, 4 people chose oranges, and the remainder chose melons, how many people chose melons?

   (A) 7
   (B) 8
   (C) 9
   (D) 10
   (E) 12

23. If the first 5 terms of a sequence are 6, 9, 14, 17, 22, then what will be the tenth term in the sequence?

   (A) 25
   (B) 41
   (C) 45
   (D) 48
   (E) 52

24. Perry is creating a garden by planting a border of bushes around a rectangular lawn, as shown. If the width of the bushes is 3 feet, what is the outer perimeter of Perry's garden, in feet?

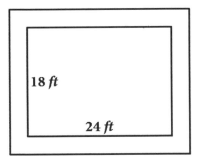

   (A) 42
   (B) 84
   (C) 96
   (D) 108
   (E) 432

CONTINUE TO THE NEXT PAGE

25. If the difference between 6 and a number h is less than 3, which of the following CANNOT be the value of h?

    (A) 9
    (B) 8
    (C) 7
    (D) 6
    (E) 5

STOP

Section 2: Reading Comprehension

40 questions
40 minutes

Directions: Read each passage in this section carefully and answer the questions that follow. Choose the best answer based on the passage.

Line 5

10

15

According to one Iroquois myth, when time began the Earth was covered by water and the people lived in a giant sky dome that was ruled by the "Great Chief." The Great Chief had a daughter, Sky Woman, whom he sent to Earth to bring light and land. On Earth, she had twin children, Sapling and Flint. Sapling was good and Flint was evil. Sapling and Flint were responsible for creating almost everything else on Earth.

The opposing forces of good and evil were a central part of Iroquois beliefs. Harmony between these two very different forces was seen as essential for maintaining a successful society. Taking responsibility for personal actions and working together with other tribe members were highly praised. Selfish acts or promoting individual benefits at the expense of the group was seen as shameful behavior.

These beliefs led to a culture of respect for both tribe members and the natural environment. The Iroquois people were noted for equal treatment of men and women. They also had a deep respect for the animals that they killed. For example, they placed restrictions on how animal bodies were to be treated after death. Deer were particularly important to the tribe. The bones of a deer were not to be fed to dogs but rather placed in trees, away from predators. The crops important to the tribe were elevated to the level of gods or spiritual beings. Corn, beans, and squash were referred to as the "three sisters," and the cycle of ceremonies was planned around the planting, growth, and harvest of the three sisters.

1. According to the passage, the Iroquois people viewed animals as

   (A) part of their society
   (B) an important food source
   (C) the source of good and evil
   (D) worthy of being treated with dignity
   (E) creatures to be feared but respected

2. It can be concluded from the passage that the "three sisters" were important to Iroquois people because they

   (A) lived in the Sky Dome
   (B) created the Sky Dome
   (C) represented good and evil
   (D) were the daughters of the Great Chief
   (E) were important to the tribes' survival

3. As used in line 6, the word "harmony" is closest in meaning to

   (A) confusion
   (B) balance
   (C) influence
   (D) music
   (E) communication

4. This passage is primarily about

   (A) how the Earth was created
   (B) tribes that live in North America
   (C) important beliefs of the Iroquois people
   (D) why actions should benefit a group and not an individual
   (E) the relationship between animals and crops in the Iroquois culture

CONTINUE TO THE NEXT PAGE

An ecosystem is a community where nonliving elements interact with living organisms. A common misunderstanding is that ecosystems are separate from human activity. However, manmade cities create urban ecosystems that are some of the most complex.

Urban ecosystems cover roughly 2% of the land surface of the Earth, but over half of the human

Line 5 population lives in one of them. There are several unique features of cities, and these affect what organisms live and thrive in them. For example, when cities are built, plants are replaced with paved surfaces like roadways and sidewalks. During the day, these dark surfaces absorb heat from the sun, and at night they release that heat back into the atmosphere. This creates heat islands in a city that are often warmer than nearby areas.

10 Urban ecosystems also have unique characteristics with regard to the movement of mass and energy. In a typical city, more materials are brought into a city than are shipped out of a city. This means that, over time, a city collects mass. Other ecosystems, such as forests, regularly experience catastrophic events such as fires that clear out accumulated mass. However, cities don't regularly experience these kinds of events. Therefore, humans must move accumulated mass to another

15 ecosystem. Urban ecosystems are also unique because most of the resources needed must be brought in from outside the boundaries of the ecosystem. There is not enough food, water, and building material generally created within the urban ecosystem to support all of its inhabitants, so these goods must come from other places.

5. According to the passage, heat islands are caused when

(A) goods are brought into a city
(B) the population of a city grows
(C) sunlight heats up an ecosystem during the day
(D) a catastrophic event such as a fire happens in a city
(E) natural materials are replaced with manmade materials

6. It can be concluded from the passage that city ecosystems

(A) cannot sustain themselves
(B) are the leading source of pollution
(C) have growing human populations
(D) tend to warm the surrounding ecosystems
(E) do not contain a diverse assortment of inhabitants

7. As used in the passage, the phrase "accumulated mass" (line 13) most likely refers to material that is

(A) consumed
(B) discarded
(C) useful
(D) decaying
(E) needed

8. It can be inferred from the passage that many people

(A) disregard human activity in ecosystems
(B) prefer not to live in urban ecosystems
(C) move into cities to avoid catastrophic events
(D) are involved in the removal of accumulated mass from a city
(E) focus on the movement of mass and energy when they study cities

9. The style of this passage is most like that of

(A) a novel
(B) a memoir
(C) an instructional manual
(D) a textbook on ecosystems
(E) a professional journal for urban planners

CONTINUE TO THE NEXT PAGE

This passage is excerpted from "How to Tell a Story" by Mark Twain.

I do not claim that I can tell a story as it ought to be told. I only claim to know how a story ought to be told, for I have been almost daily in the company of the most expert story-tellers for many years.

There are several kinds of stories, but only one difficult kind—the humorous. I will talk mainly
Line 5 about that one. The humorous story is American, the comic story is English, the witty story is French. The humorous story depends for its effect upon the manner of the telling; the comic story and the witty story upon the matter.

The humorous story may be spun out to great length, and may wander around as much as it pleases, and arrive nowhere in particular; but the comic and witty stories must be brief and end
10 with a point. The humorous story bubbles gently along, the others burst.

The humorous story is strictly a work of art—high and delicate art—and only an artist can tell it; but no art is necessary in telling the comic and the witty story; anybody can do it. The art of telling a humorous story—understand, I mean by word of mouth, not print—was created in America, and has remained at home.

15 The humorous story is told gravely; the teller does his best to conceal the fact that he even dimly suspects that there is anything funny about it; but the teller of the comic story tells you beforehand that it is one of the funniest things he has ever heard, then tells it with eager delight, and is the first person to laugh when he gets through. And sometimes, if he has had good success, he is so glad and happy that he will repeat the "nub" of it and glance around from face to face,
20 collecting applause, and then repeat it again. It is a pathetic thing to see.

Very often, of course, the rambling and disjointed humorous story finishes with a nub, point, snapper, or whatever you like to call it. Then the listener must be alert, for in many cases the teller will divert attention from that nub by dropping it in a carefully casual and indifferent way, with the pretense that he does not know it is a nub.

10. The attitude of the author towards comic stories can best be described as

(A) curious
(B) admiring
(C) disdainful
(D) impatient
(E) exhausted

11. It can be inferred from the passage that, as compared to witty and comic stories, humorous stories

(A) tend to be of greater length
(B) come only from one country
(C) end with a nub or a snapper
(D) are more likely to produce applause
(E) are not easily recognized by the listener

12. According to the passage, humorous stories rely more upon

(A) a strict format
(B) the number of times a story has been told
(C) how quickly the storyteller can get to the point
(D) how the story is told and not the content of the story
(E) an audience that does not expect what the ending will be

13. The author believes that a humorous storyteller should

(A) ignore his audience
(B) make his story more brief
(C) wait for the audience reaction
(D) never tell a story more than once
(E) not reveal that he finds the story humorous

CONTINUE TO THE NEXT PAGE

14. Which best states the main idea of this passage?

   (A) Humorous stories are uniquely American.
   (B) The narrator believes himself to be a superior storyteller.
   (C) Humorous stories are an art form that is superior to witty or comic stories.
   (D) Rambling and jumbled stories are best categorized as being humorous stories.
   (E) Those who tell comic or witty stories are often trying to tell humorous stories but fall short.

The aye-aye is one of the world's most unusual animals. It is a lemur that lives in Madagascar. Aye-ayes spend most of their lives in trees and are the largest nocturnal primates in the world. They are known for teeth that are constantly growing and for an exceptionally long, narrow middle finger. They mainly feed on grubs or beetles. Aye-ayes will tap on trees to find their prey, use their

Line 5   incisor teeth to poke a hole in the bark, and then extract the grubs with their long middle finger. This feeding strategy is very similar to that of the woodpecker.

The aye-ayes have a nocturnal lifestyle. They have large, beady eyes that help them see in the dark. They are also somewhat fearless about coming into contact with human beings. Because of their habits of prowling the trees at night and of frequently approaching humans with their

10   penetrating glare, they are often featured as villains in folk tales. One myth told by some villagers in Madagascar is that if an aye-aye points its long middle finger at you, then you are marked for death. The only way to avoid this fate is to kill the aye-aye. Unfortunately, this superstition, combined with the destruction of their habitat and poaching by farmers, has led to aye-ayes being identified as an endangered species. If protective measures are not taken, aye-ayes could disappear

15   completely.

---

15. The author most likely mentions woodpeckers to

   (A) contrast birds and other animals
   (B) compare the aye-aye to a more familiar animal
   (C) describe how another nocturnal animal captures prey
   (D) show how two frequently confused animals are different
   (E) inform the reader how woodpeckers feed

16. It can be inferred from the passage that some villagers in Madagascar view aye-ayes as a

   (A) threat
   (B) nuisance
   (C) sign of good fortune
   (D) reminder of the past
   (E) temptation for poachers

17. As used in line 5, the word "extract" is closest in meaning to

   (A) eat
   (B) remove
   (C) fasten
   (D) notice
   (E) postpone

18. The author's tone can best be described as

   (A) soothing
   (B) desperate
   (C) disinterested
   (D) optimistic
   (E) concerned

19. The primary purpose of this passage is most likely to

   (A) describe endangered animals
   (B) criticize the people of Madagascar
   (C) give readers an awareness of aye-ayes and the threats they face
   (D) detail unique characteristics of nocturnal animals
   (E) inform the reader how aye-ayes differ from other animals

CONTINUE TO THE NEXT PAGE

This passage is taken from the autobiography of naturalist Charles Darwin.

I have heard my father and elder sister say that I had, as a very young boy, a strong taste for long solitary walks; but what I thought about I know not. I often became quite absorbed, and once, whilst returning to school on the summit of the old fortifications round Shrewsbury, which had been converted into a public foot-path with no parapet on one side, I walked off and fell to the

Line 5 ground, but the height was only seven or eight feet. Nevertheless the number of thoughts which passed through my mind during this very short, but sudden and wholly unexpected fall, was astonishing, and seem hardly compatible with what physiologists have, I believe, proved about each thought requiring quite an appreciable amount of time.

Nothing could have been worse for the development of my mind than Dr. Butler's school, as

10 it was strictly classical, nothing else being taught, except a little ancient geography and history. The school as a means of education to me was simply a blank. During my whole life I have been singularly incapable of mastering any language. Especial attention was paid to verse-making, and this I could never do well. I had many friends, and got together a good collection of old verses, which by patching together, sometimes aided by other boys, I could work into any subject. Much

15 attention was paid to learning by heart the lessons of the previous day; this I could effect with great facility, learning forty or fifty lines of Virgil or Homer, whilst I was in morning chapel; but this exercise was utterly useless, for every verse was forgotten in forty-eight hours. I was not idle, and with the exception of versification, generally worked conscientiously at my classics, not using cribs. The sole pleasure I ever received from such studies, was from some of the odes of Horace, which I

20 admired greatly.

When I left the school I was for my age neither high nor low in it; and I believe that I was considered by all my masters and by my father as a very ordinary boy, rather below the common standard in intellect. To my deep mortification my father once said to me, "You care for nothing but shooting, dogs, and rat-catching, and you will be a disgrace to yourself and all your family."

20. The narrator of this passage believes that memorizing classical texts is

(A) extremely difficult
(B) important for some students
(C) best done with a group of friends
(D) not valuable for developing thinking skills
(E) a sign that a student has too much idle time

21. In the first paragraph, the narrator describes himself as

(A) careful to the extreme
(B) suspicious of other people
(C) not a very talented student
(D) disliked by his father and sister
(E) consumed with his own thoughts

22. Which word could be substituted for "mortification" (line 23) and maintain the meaning of the sentence?

(A) interest
(B) nausea
(C) boredom
(D) embarrassment
(E) satisfaction

23. From the details in the passage, it can be inferred that the narrator's father

(A) prefers his daughter to his son
(B) is the head of the narrator's school
(C) does not value knowledge of the natural world
(D) was successful in school as a young child
(E) wants his son to only study ancient geography and history

CONTINUE TO THE NEXT PAGE

24. The author's tone when describing his school can best be described as

(A) weary and discouraged
(B) sensitive and engaged
(C) restless and offended
(D) anxious and cooperative
(E) inquisitive and energetic

On her first day at the new school, Susan nervously approached the rusty gate, glancing at the blacktop that stretched out before her like a minefield to be crossed. She knew that it was a critical first test to make it through the schoolyard and to the door without attracting attention. She walked cautiously through the gate, keeping her head down as she shuffled as quickly as she could

Line 5   across the hot, black tar.

Just when Susan thought she had made it, a rubber ball hit her left arm, sending her books scattering. She had attended enough new schools to know that this was not a good sign. She tensed, waiting for the bully to follow the ball.

Suddenly, one of the oddest children she had ever seen bounced into view. This girl had a mop

10   of curly hair trying desperately to free itself from a striped ribbon. Her denim overalls were cut off at the knees, showcasing the mismatched socks she wore pulled up to her knees.

When she saw the terrified look on Susan's face, she threw back her head and laughed with a vibration that came straight from her belly. It was probably the most joyous noise that Susan had ever heard.

25. In line 10, the phrase "curly hair trying desperately to free itself" is an example of

(A) allusion
(B) personification
(C) foreshadowing
(D) euphemism
(E) hyperbole

26. Based on information in the passage, Susan can best be described as

(A) cruel
(B) scornful
(C) outgoing
(D) abrasive
(E) apprehensive

27. In this passage, the author's primary purpose is to

(A) offer advice
(B) describe two characters
(C) describe the setting of a story
(D) introduce a sense of suspense
(E) convince the reader to take action

28. The most important function of the first paragraph is to

(A) emphasize how hot a day it was
(B) explain how new students are treated
(C) give insight into how a character feels
(D) provide information about Susan's school
(E) introduce the reader to the setting of a story

29. Which of the following is a synonym for the word "critical" as used in line 3?

(A) demanding
(B) negative
(C) cautious
(D) significant
(E) hopeful

CONTINUE TO THE NEXT PAGE

It is a duty of national journalism to assist in the organization of public opinion. No matter what particular department of civilization may for the moment be under the need of assistance, still the journal of public usefulness is under obligation to try to help.

Just now the department of civilization that appears to be of more importance to the world
Line 5 than all other departments combined is the ancient, homely, unromantic department of "Good Samaritanism"- the elementary and ofttimes criticized work of right-hearted people- of feeding the hungry and clothing the naked.

This magazine has been invited to help in this simple program of humanitarianism by appealing to its readers and in turn inviting their help.

10 Pearson's has responded to many calls for the help of its power of publicity. Its readers are by no means numerically of the strongest of all magazine families; but in national spirit, it is doubtful if any organized group can show the high percentage of effectiveness that Pearson's readers have shown in the past- whenever they have been given an opportunity to serve the common good.

30. Based on information in the passage, the author believes that journalists have a unique responsibility to

(A) encourage readers to help the less fortunate
(B) personally perform acts of humanitarian service
(C) spread the word about individual acts of "Good Samaritanism"
(D) provide criticism of people who take advantage of those in need
(E) try to get readers to compete with one another to perform charitable acts

31. The passage implies that "Good Samaritanism" is often

(A) underappreciated
(B) a source of debate
(C) overly complicated
(D) dramatically described
(E) motivated for the wrong purposes

32. 25. As used in the passage, the word "publicity" (line 10) is closest in meaning to

(A) label
(B) promotion
(C) nervousness
(D) disagreement
(E) requirement

33. The author's tone can best be described as

(A) ironic
(B) sarcastic
(C) humorous
(D) resigned
(E) earnest

34. The passage suggests that the readers of Pearson's magazine are

(A) careless about their duties
(B) more numerous than the readers of other magazines
(C) more likely to help others than readers of other magazines
(D) difficult to convince but ultimately pull through when help is needed
(E) known to spread the word when they hear of a humanitarian cause

35. The author of this passage is primarily concerned with

(A) explaining the role of journalism
(B) persuading readers to take action
(C) finding a solution to homelessness
(D) reprimanding readers of other magazines
(E) describing ways that readers can help others

CONTINUE TO THE NEXT PAGE

The age of Vikings lasted from about the late 8th century to the 11th century. The Vikings lived in Scandinavia and were expert sailors who journeyed far and wide. They had distinctive boats that were designed to sail across oceans but also to be rowed into battle. Their boats often had unique scrollwork on the front and back that gave them an appearance like a sea creature ready to charge.

Line 5   The Vikings were famous for their raids along coastlines. In addition, they travelled looking to establish trade routes.

There is much debate among historians about the reasons that the Vikings sailed. Many of the sailors were farmers who would travel in the summer while their wives would tend the farms back home. The Scandinavian landscape was harsh and it was difficult to grow enough food to support

10   the population. Viking sailors would return before winter with their boats full of supplies to help their families survive the unrelenting winters.

During the Viking Age, the Scandinavian people controlled much of Northern Europe and raids were reported in a far larger area. The furthest recorded journey of the Vikings was to Baghdad. In Baghdad, they would trade goods such as fur, tusks, and seal fat. There is also

15   evidence that they made it as far west as North America. Scientists have been working to uncover possible evidence of Viking life in Newfoundland, which is located on the eastern coast of Canada.

36. According to the passage, all of the following were true about Vikings EXCEPT they

(A) sailed to North America
(B) were known for raids along shorelines
(C) stayed home to farm during the summer
(D) were interested in setting up trade routes
(E) lived in an area with poor farming conditions

37. Which technique does the author use to describe Viking boats?

(A) simile
(B) hyperbole
(C) allusion
(D) personification
(E) synecdoche

38. The word "unrelenting" (line 11) could be replaced with which word without changing the meaning of the sentence?

(A) temperate
(B) unpredictable
(C) subtle
(D) merciless
(E) languishing

39. This passage would most likely be found in a

(A) novel
(B) literary anthology
(C) history textbook
(D) traveler's diary
(E) science textbook

40. Which best summarizes the main idea of this passage?

(A) Vikings are known for being cruel raiders.
(B) It is very difficult to support a family in Scandinavia.
(C) Vikings turned to sailing because of poor farming conditions.
(D) There was much political upheaval in the 8th to 11th centuries.
(E) Viking sailors travelled far and wide during the 8th to 11th centuries.

STOP

Section 3: Verbal

60 questions
30 minutes

This section has two types of questions – synonyms and analogies.

Synonyms

Directions: Each question has a word in all capital letters and then five answer choices that are in lower case letters. Choose the answer choice that has the word (or phrase) that is closest in meaning to the word that is in capital letters.

1. EXHIBIT:

   (A) fascinate
   (B) object
   (C) present
   (D) sling
   (E) defy

2. REMARK:

   (A) comment
   (B) embarrassment
   (C) spectacle
   (D) manuscript
   (E) illustration

3. ENCHANT:

   (A) surpass
   (B) arrange
   (C) recite
   (D) imitate
   (E) delight

4. PRIMARY:

   (A) most important
   (B) lacking detail
   (C) outdated
   (D) suddenly stopped
   (E) minor

5. EMPLOY:

   (A) suggest
   (B) contact
   (C) hesitate
   (D) test
   (E) use

6. OPPOSITION:

   (A) receipt
   (B) emphasis
   (C) resistance
   (D) division
   (E) profession

CONTINUE TO THE NEXT PAGE

7. PARCHED:

   (A) tangled
   (B) scorched
   (C) crooked
   (D) failing
   (E) weathered

8. REALM:

   (A) theory
   (B) galaxy
   (C) shelter
   (D) ornament
   (E) territory

9. JUBILANT:

   (A) subdued
   (B) familiar
   (C) joyous
   (D) willing
   (E) healthy

10. ACUTE:

    (A) elevated
    (B) refined
    (C) talented
    (D) incomplete
    (E) intense

11. HARDY:

    (A) tough
    (B) active
    (C) imaginary
    (D) valuable
    (E) final

12. DISREGARD:

    (A) persuade
    (B) ignore
    (C) transmit
    (D) adjust
    (E) engage

13. TAILOR:

    (A) customize
    (B) support
    (C) elaborate
    (D) match
    (E) leave

14. ENDEAVOR:

    (A) mainstay
    (B) series
    (C) venture
    (D) form
    (E) reputation

15. ABNORMAL:

    (A) dainty
    (B) twisted
    (C) gradual
    (D) peculiar
    (E) homely

16. FLOUNDER:

    (A) lessen
    (B) transform
    (C) glorify
    (D) evaporate
    (E) stumble

17. TAUNT:

    (A) uphold
    (B) punish
    (C) ridicule
    (D) trick
    (E) misplace

18. DIVULGE:

    (A) flee
    (B) reveal
    (C) scheme
    (D) improve
    (E) locate

CONTINUE TO THE NEXT PAGE

19. RELIABLE:

(A) trustworthy
(B) horrified
(C) limp
(D) courteous
(E) original

20. DAUNTLESS:

(A) proper
(B) courageous
(C) absent
(D) just
(E) majestic

21. ENTICE:

(A) measure
(B) judge
(C) startle
(D) crush
(E) tempt

22. SUBLIME:

(A) humane
(B) illustrious
(C) regrettable
(D) magnificent
(E) dreary

23. FRAY:

(A) battle
(B) instant
(C) mixture
(D) grade
(E) settlement

24. MORTIFY:

(A) stop
(B) drag
(C) embarrass
(D) position
(E) smear

25. PREHISTORIC:

(A) enthusiastic
(B) rugged
(C) enclosed
(D) dingy
(E) ancient

26. PLAUSIBLE:

(A) decisive
(B) believable
(C) hasty
(D) definite
(E) seldom

27. LISTLESS:

(A) without substance
(B) without liquid
(C) without thought
(D) without energy
(E) without hunger

28. RUSE:

(A) hoax
(B) medley
(C) profit
(D) foe
(E) farewell

29. DIFFUSE:

(A) scattered
(B) critical
(C) rotten
(D) soaked
(E) tattered

30. DEPLETE:

(A) slice
(B) contribute
(C) exhaust
(D) preserve
(E) remind

CONTINUE TO THE NEXT PAGE

Analogies

Directions: Identify the relationships between the words. Then choose the answer choice that best finishes the sentence.

31. Boat is to ferry as

    (A) rabbit is to hare
    (B) garment is to shirt
    (C) water is to ocean
    (D) fork is to dish
    (E) soccer is to field

32. Horse is to carriage as oxen is to

    (A) cow
    (B) tadpole
    (C) truck
    (D) trailer
    (E) plow

33. Gallon is to volume as

    (A) yard is to length
    (B) inch is to foot
    (C) page is to book
    (D) cup is to quart
    (E) water is to jug

34. Accident is to careless as

    (A) king is to friendly
    (B) word is to ready
    (C) onion is to smelly
    (D) success is to industrious
    (E) excuse is to honest

35. Factory is to goods as

    (A) meadow is to flowers
    (B) hospital is to doctor
    (C) sweater is to wool
    (D) bakery is to bread
    (E) depot is to locomotive

36. Students is to class as

    (A) musicians is to violin
    (B) saplings is to tree
    (C) timbers is to lodge
    (D) fountains is to plaza
    (E) teachers is to faculty

37. Customer is to buy as

    (A) farmer is to market
    (B) neighbor is to mail
    (C) soldier is to defend
    (D) inventor is to property
    (E) supervisor is to department

38. Pit is to peach as

    (A) rind is to melon
    (B) pulp is to orange
    (C) juice is to grapefruit
    (D) core is to apple
    (E) lime is to lemon

39. Education is to academy as

    (A) experiments is to laboratory
    (B) prisoner is to jail
    (C) greeting is to monarch
    (D) heap is to garbage
    (E) parachute is to airplane

40. Opinion is to argument as evidence is to

    (A) routine
    (B) theory
    (C) repetition
    (D) nature
    (E) solution

CONTINUE TO THE NEXT PAGE

41. Fox is to den as groundhog is to

   (A) corral
   (B) forest
   (C) pup
   (D) burrow
   (E) quill

42. Jacket is to warm as

   (A) suit is to casual
   (B) hat is to sunny
   (C) poncho is to dry
   (D) strap is to heavy
   (E) pants is to long

43. Dough is to bread as

   (A) pavement is to tar
   (B) fruit is to juice
   (C) trees is to grove
   (D) pretzel is to mustard
   (E) display is to product

44. Acrobat is to trapeze as

   (A) captain is to ship
   (B) umpire is to baseball
   (C) chemist is to potion
   (D) principal is to car
   (E) astronaut is to spacecraft

45. Slippery is to ice as

   (A) graceful is to dancer
   (B) brief is to skit
   (C) frozen is to mine
   (D) rough is to sandpaper
   (E) immense is to building

46. Lettuce is to produce as milk is to

   (A) waves
   (B) dairy
   (C) penny
   (D) pair
   (E) river

47. Joke is to laughter as

   (A) broadcast is to listen
   (B) comparison is to winner
   (C) pain is to grimace
   (D) ticket is to show
   (E) course is to grade

48. Statue is to stone as

   (A) cougar is to prey
   (B) pot is to clay
   (C) clothes is to outfit
   (D) entrance is to doorman
   (E) shower is to bath

49. Scarlet is to color as

   (A) pattern is to blocks
   (B) reservation is to restaurant
   (C) message is to record
   (D) toast is to bread
   (E) basil is to herb

50. Moist is to soaking as warm is to

   (A) sweltering
   (B) clouded
   (C) resting
   (D) faithful
   (E) ordinary

51. Prosperous is to wealthy as

   (A) forgotten is to remembered
   (B) crash is to mess
   (C) valor is to courage
   (D) kind is to responsible
   (E) feast is to meal

52. Avalanche is to flurries as

   (A) bench is to seat
   (B) trowel is to shovel
   (C) lullaby is to sleep
   (D) canyon is to trench
   (E) event is to spectator

CONTINUE TO THE NEXT PAGE

53. Gloomy is to weather as

    (A)   cranky is to mood

    (B)   green is to suburb

    (C)   round is to diameter

    (D)   secure is to rope

    (E)   nervous is to fright

54. Landlord is to housing as

    (A)   hiker is to trail

    (B)   professor is to college

    (C)   police is to protection

    (D)   stranger is to meet

    (E)   warrior is to weapon

55. Refuse is to decline as

    (A)   abandon is to transfer

    (B)   capture is to trap

    (C)   imitate is to act

    (D)   flutter is to bond

    (E)   sterilize is to clean

56. Band is to banned as

    (A)   flute is to instrument

    (B)   cell is to sell

    (C)   orchestra is to conductor

    (D)   tablet is to table

    (E)   steak is to beef

57. Anxious is to serenity as

    (A)   pious is to belief

    (B)   loyal is to companion

    (C)   arrogant is to humility

    (D)   delicate is to structure

    (E)   cautious is to destination

58. Hoarse is to voice as

    (A)   professional is to job

    (B)   strained is to muscles

    (C)   guilty is to crime

    (D)   devoted is to commitment

    (E)   hardy is to mass

59. Skillful is to expert as inept is to

    (A)   human

    (B)   sherrlf

    (C)   novice

    (D)   sheperd

    (E)   typist

60. Concealed is to obvious as

    (A)   disqualified is to eliminated

    (B)   intact is to glamorous

    (C)   flimsy is to soft

    (D)   admired is to disliked

    (E)   glinting is to shiny

STOP

Section 4: Quantitative

25 questions
30 minutes

Directions: Each problem is followed by five answer choices. Solve each problem and then decide which answer choice is best.

---

1. In a bag of marbles, there are 4 green marbles, 8 red marbles, and 13 blue marbles. If a marble is chosen at random, what is the probability that a green marble will be chosen?

    (A) $\dfrac{4}{25}$

    (B) $\dfrac{8}{25}$

    (C) $\dfrac{1}{4}$

    (D) $\dfrac{1}{3}$

    (E) $\dfrac{1}{2}$

CONTINUE TO THE NEXT PAGE

2. The graph below shows the distance from a garage for four different cars versus time. In the time period shown, which car travelled the greatest distance?

Distance from garage by time of day

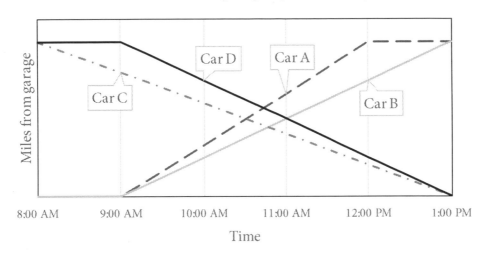

(A)   Car A
(B)   Car B
(C)   Car C
(D)   Car D
(E)   all the cars travelled the same distance

CONTINUE TO THE NEXT PAGE

3. Tabitha purchased a tennis racket for $145 and several cans of tennis balls for $3.25 for each can. If the total amount of money that Tabitha spent can be determined using the expression $145 + 3.25m$, what does m represent?

    (A) the cost for each can of tennis balls
    (B) the total cost of the racket and the tennis balls
    (C) the number of cans of tennis balls
    (D) the number of rackets
    (E) the cost for the racket

4. What is the value of $1,051 + 347 - 594$?

    (A) 110
    (B) 704
    (C) 794
    (D) 804
    (E) 1,992

5. Esther surveyed 450 people and asked them if they owned a scooter or a bicycle. If all of the respondents owned either a bicycle or a scooter, 324 people responded that they owned a bicycle, and 188 people responded that they owned a scooter, then how many people must have responded that they owned both a bicycle and a scooter?

    (A) 262
    (B) 136
    (C) 124
    (D) 126
    (E) 62

6. Which ratio is equivalent to the ratio 2 to 5?

    (A) 4 to 25
    (B) 6 to 15
    (C) 6 to 25
    (D) 8 to 25
    (E) 20 to 4

CONTINUE TO THE NEXT PAGE

7. What is the value of 0.92 divided by 1,000?

    (A) 0.00092
    (B) 0.0092
    (C) 0.092
    (D) 0.92
    (E) 9.2

8. Kendra has twice as many books as Lynne does. If they have a total of 54 books, how many books does Lynne have?

    (A) 18
    (B) 27
    (C) 30
    (D) 36
    (E) 42

9. If each class in a school has exactly 18 students, which could be the total number of students at this school?

    (A) 218
    (B) 234
    (C) 250
    (D) 254
    (E) 263

10. On a particular test, twenty students answered 80% or more of the questions correctly. Eight students answered 90% or more of the questions correctly. How many students answered at least 80% but less than 90% of the questions correctly?

    (A) 8
    (B) 10
    (C) 12
    (D) 20
    (E) 28

CONTINUE TO THE NEXT PAGE

Questions 11-12 are based on the line graph that shows how many miles a truck driver had driven from his home base over the course of a day.

Distance from home base by time of day

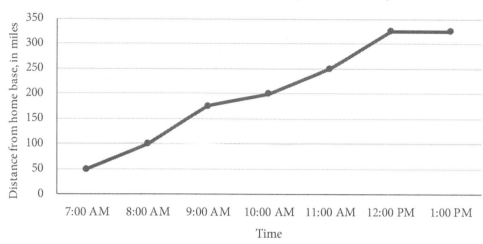

11. How many more miles did the truck driver drive between 11 AM and 12 PM than between 9 AM and 10 AM?

    (A) 20
    (B) 50
    (C) 105
    (D) 125
    (E) 145

12. The driver was how many more miles from his home base at 1 PM than he was at 7 AM?

    (A) 50
    (B) 275
    (C) 300
    (D) 325
    (E) 350

CONTINUE TO THE NEXT PAGE

13. Which is the value of $12 \times 6 \div 8$?

    (A) $\dfrac{1}{4}$

    (B)   9

    (C)   15

    (D)   16

    (E)   72

14. If $\dfrac{n}{9}$ is a whole number, which of the following could be the value of n?

    (A)   763

    (B)   784

    (C)   786

    (D)   792

    (E)   804

15. The length of a rectangle is twice as long as its width. If the width of the rectangle is represented by w, then which expression represents the area of the rectangle?

    (A) $4w$

    (B) $4w^2$

    (C) $2w$

    (D) $2w + 2$

    (E) $2w^2$

16. Sue has put stamps on $\dfrac{2}{5}$ of the envelopes that she needs to put stamps on. If she has put stamps on 36 envelopes, how many more envelopes must she put stamps on?

    (A)   18

    (B)   54

    (C)   72

    (D)   90

    (E)   108

CONTINUE TO THE NEXT PAGE

17.   What is the value of 0.21 × 0.03?

    (A)   0.0063
    (B)   0.063
    (C)   0.073
    (D)   0.63
    (E)   6.3

18.   Which expression is NOT equivalent to 312 + (45 × 12 × 23)?

    (A)   312 + (45 × 12) × 23
    (B)   312 + 45 × (12 × 23)
    (C)   (312 + 45) × 12 × 23
    (D)   312 + (12 × 45 × 23)
    (E)   312 + 45 × 12 × 23

19.   What is the value of 16 − 4 × 5 + 3?

    (A)   −1
    (B)   1
    (C)   45
    (D)   61
    (E)   63

20.   Sheryl is younger than Veronica and Roderick. Devin is older than Sheryl. Veronica is younger than Devin. Who is oldest?

    (A)   Sheryl
    (B)   Veronica
    (C)   Roderick
    (D)   Devin
    (E)   Cannot be determined from information given

21.   The area of the base of a prism is 8 square inches and the height of the prism is 10 inches. What is the volume of this prism, in cubic inches?

    (A)   18
    (B)   40
    (C)   64
    (D)   80
    (E)   640

CONTINUE TO THE NEXT PAGE

22.　On Tuesday, Daryl collected 40 cans for recycling. On Wednesday, he collected 50 cans for recycling. The number of cans he collected on Wednesday was what percent greater than the number of cans he collected on Tuesday?

(A)　20%
(B)　25%
(C)　33%
(D)　40%
(E)　50%

23.　For every 3 caramels, there are 5 chocolates in a container. If there are a total of 112 caramels and chocolates in the container, how many caramels are there?

(A)　8
(B)　9
(C)　14
(D)　28
(E)　42

24.　If $y - 5 = 6y$, then what is the value of y?

(A)　−1
(B)　0
(C)　1
(D)　2
(E)　5

25.　In the figure shown, lines b and c are parallel and are intersected by line d. What is the value of $x + y$?

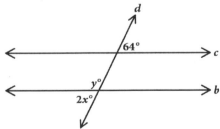

(A)　64
(B)　74
(C)　148
(D)　164
(E)　180

STOP

———

———

The Best Unofficial Practice Tests for the Middle Level SSAT

———

Practice Test 1, Section 1 – Quantitative

Correct Answer	Your Answer	Put a check mark here if you answered the question correctly
1. B		
2. C		
3. C		
4. E		
5. D		
6. C		
7. B		
8. B		
9. D		
10. A		
11. E		
12. D		
13. B		
14. C		
15. C		
16. C		
17. A		
18. A		
19. E		
20. C		
21. D		
22. C		
23. B		
24. A		
25. B		
Total Questions Answered Correctly _____		

Practice Test 1, Section 2 – Reading Comprehension

Correct Answer	Your Answer	Put a check mark here if you answered the question correctly
1. B		
2. B		
3. C		
4. C		
5. D		
6. A		
7. C		
8. C		
9. B		
10. E		
11. C		
12. C		
13. A		
14. D		
15. B		
16. A		
17. D		
18. B		
19. B		
20. E		
21. A		
22. D		
23. A		
24. D		
25. A		
26. E		
27. E		
28. E		
29. A		
30. E		
31. B		
32. A		
33. D		
34. A		

35. B		
36. C		
37. B		
38. A		
39. E		
40. D		
Total Questions Answered Correctly _____		

Practice Test 1, Section 3 – Verbal

Correct Answer	Your Answer	Put a check mark here if you answered the question correctly
1. B		
2. E		
3. A		
4. D		
5. C		
6. E		
7. B		
8. A		
9. C		
10. D		
11. E		
12. A		
13. B		
14. C		
15. D		
16. B		
17. A		
18. E		
19. B		
20. C		
21. D		
22. A		
23. B		
24. E		
25. C		
26. D		
27. B		
28. A		
29. E		
30. B		
31. E		
32. A		
33. B		
34. D		

35.C		
36.B		
37.E		
38.A		
39.B		
40.A		
41.D		
42.B		
43.C		
44.A		
45.E		
46.C		
47.A		
48.B		
49.D		
50.E		
51.A		
52.C		
53.B		
54.B		
55.A		
56.D		
57.E		
58.D		
59.B		
60.C		
Total Questions Answered Correctly _____		

_____

Practice Test 1, Section 4 – Quantitative

Correct Answer	Your Answer	Put a check mark here if you answered the question correctly
1. D		
2. B		
3. A		
4. B		
5. E		
6. D		
7. B		
8. C		
9. D		
10. D		
11. E		
12. B		
13. B		
14. E		
15. C		
16. D		
17. C		
18. B		
19. A		
20. E		
21. C		
22. A		
23. D		
24. E		
25. E		
Total Questions Answered Correctly _____		

_____

Practice Test 2, Section 1 – Quantitative

Correct Answer	Your Answer	Put a check mark here if you answered the question correctly
1. D		
2. D		
3. E		
4. A		
5. D		
6. C		
7. B		
8. A		
9. B		
10. C		
11. D		
12. E		
13. E		
14. C		
15. B		
16. E		
17. B		
18. A		
19. C		
20. D		
21. C		
22. A		
23. B		
24. D		
25. A		
Total Questions Answered Correctly _____		

Practice Test 2, Section 2 – Reading Comprehension

Correct Answer	Your Answer	Put a check mark here if you answered the question correctly
1. D		
2. E		
3. B		
4. C		
5. E		
6. A		
7. B		
8. A		
9. D		
10. C		
11. A		
12. D		
13. E		
14. C		
15. B		
16. A		
17. B		
18. E		
19. C		
20. D		
21. E		
22. D		
23. C		
24. A		
25. B		
26. E		
27. B		
28. C		
29. D		
30. A		
31. A		
32. B		
33. E		
34. C		

35.B		
36.C		
37.A		
38.D		
39.C		
40.E		
Total Questions Answered Correctly _____		

Practice Test 2, Section 3 – Verbal

Correct Answer	Your Answer	Put a check mark here if you answered the question correctly
1. C		
2. A		
3. E		
4. A		
5. E		
6. C		
7. B		
8. E		
9. C		
10. E		
11. A		
12. B		
13. A		
14. C		
15. D		
16. E		
17. C		
18. B		
19. A		
20. B		
21. E		
22. D		
23. A		
24. C		
25. E		
26. B		
27. D		
28. A		
29. A		
30. C		
31. B		
32. E		
33. A		
34. D		

35.D		
36.E		
37.C		
38.D		
39.A		
40.B		
41.D		
42.C		
43.B		
44.E		
45.D		
46.B		
47.C		
48.B		
49.E		
50.A		
51.C		
52.D		
53.A		
54.C		
55.E		
56.B		
57.C		
58.B		
59.C		
60.D		
Total Questions Answered Correctly _____		

Practice Test 2, Section 4 – Quantitative

Correct Answer	Your Answer	Put a check mark here if you answered the question correctly
1. A		
2. E		
3. C		
4. D		
5. E		
6. B		
7. A		
8. A		
9. B		
10. C		
11. B		
12. B		
13. B		
14. D		
15. E		
16. B		
17. A		
18. C		
19. A		
20. E		
21. D		
22. B		
23. E		
24. A		
25. C		
Total Questions Answered Correctly _____		

Interpreting your scores

On the SSAT, your raw score is the number of questions that you answered correctly on each section minus the number of questions you answered incorrectly divided by 4. Nothing is added or subtracted for the questions that you omit. Your raw score is then converted into a scaled score. This scaled score is then converted into a percentile score. Remember that it is the percentile score that schools are looking at. Your percentile score compares you only to other students in your grade. Below is a chart that gives a very rough conversion between your raw score on the practice test and a percentile score.

> PLEASE NOTE – The purpose of this chart is to let you see how the scoring works, not to give you an accurate percentile score. You will need to complete the practice test in *The Official Guide to the Middle Level SSAT* in order to get a more accurate percentile score.

Grade 5

	Section 1 + Section 4: Quantitative	Section 2: Reading comprehension	Section 3: Verbal
Approximate raw score for 75th percentile	28-29	22-23	28-29
Approximate raw score for 50th percentile	19-20	17-18	19-20
Approximate raw score for 25th percentile	11-12	11-12	12-13

Grade 6

	Section 1 + Section 4: Quantitative	Section 2: Reading comprehension	Section 3: Verbal
Approximate raw score for 75th percentile	35-36	27-28	36-37
Approximate raw score for 50th percentile	26-27	21-22	26-27
Approximate raw score for 25th percentile	16-17	14-15	17-18

Grade 7

	Section 1 + Section 4: Quantitative	Section 2: Reading comprehension	Section 3: Verbal
Approximate raw score for 75th percentile	39-40	29-30	42-43
Approximate raw score for 50th percentile	32-33	24-25	32-33
Approximate raw score for 25th percentile	22-23	17-18	23-24

Looking for more instruction and practice?

Check out our other book for the Middle Level SSAT:

Success on the Middle Level SSAT: A Complete Course

- ✓ Strategies specific to each section of the test

- ✓ Reading and vocabulary drills

- ✓ In-depth math content instruction with practice sets

Was **The Best Unofficial Practice Tests for the Middle Level SSAT** helpful to you?
Please consider leaving a review with the merchant where you purchased the book.
We welcome your suggestions at *feedback@testprepworks.com*.

Books by Test Prep Works

	Content instruction	Test-taking strategies	Practice problems	Full-length practice tests
ISEE				
Lower Level (for students applying for admission to grades 5-6)				
Success on the Lower Level ISEE	✓	✓	✓	✓ (1)
30 Days to Acing the Lower Level ISEE		✓	✓	
The Best Unofficial Practice Tests for the Lower Level ISEE				✓ (2)
Middle Level (for students applying for admission to grades 7-8)				
Success on the Middle Level ISEE	✓	✓	✓	✓ (1)
The Best Unofficial Practice Tests for the Middle Level ISEE				✓ (2)
Upper Level (for students applying for admission to grades 9-12)				
Success on the Upper Level ISEE	✓	✓	✓	✓ (1)
The Best Unofficial Practice Tests for the Upper Level ISEE				✓ (2)
SSAT				
Middle Level (for students applying for admission to grades 6-8)				
Success on the Middle Level SSAT	✓	✓	✓	
The Best Unofficial Practice Tests for the Middle Level SSAT				✓ (2)
Upper Level (for students applying for admission to grades 9-12)				
Success on the Upper Level SSAT	✓	✓	✓	✓ (1)
30 Days to Acing the Upper Level SSAT		✓	✓	
The Best Unofficial Practice Tests for the Upper Level SSAT				✓ (2)

TEST PREP WORKS, LLC.

Made in the USA
San Bernardino, CA
17 September 2018